## The Art of Great Speech
## and why we remember them

What makes a great speech 'great'?

*The Art of Great Speeches* uses insights from classical thinkers to reveal how great orators such as Barack Obama, Martin Luther King, the Kennedys, Al Gore and Hitler persuaded their audiences with such conviction.

Featuring excerpts from 70 of the world's greatest and most controversial speeches in history and drama, this fascinating book breaks down the key elements of classical and modern oratory to reveal the rhetorical techniques that make them so memorable. It shows how master speechwriters connect with their audiences, seize a moment, project character, use facts convincingly and destroy their opponents' arguments as they try to force the hand of history or create memorable drama.

Part history, part defence of oratory, part call for political inspiration, part handbook, *The Art of Great Speeches* does what no other book does – it explains *why* these speeches are great.

**Dennis Glover** is a professional speechwriter for some of Australia's most prominent political and business leaders, and an academic historian of oratory. He is a graduate of Monash University, and he took a PhD in History at Cambridge University. He has worked on the staff of three federal Labor Party leaders and written speeches for two prime ministers.

*Ex libris*

*Michael J Kelly*

# The Art of Great Speeches
# and why we remember them

Dennis Glover

CAMBRIDGE
UNIVERSITY PRESS

CAMBRIDGE UNIVERSITY PRESS
Cambridge, New York, Melbourne, Madrid, Cape Town, Singapore,
São Paulo, Delhi, Dubai, Tokyo, Mexico City

Cambridge University Press
477 Williamstown Road, Port Melbourne, VIC 3207, Australia

Published in the United States of America by Cambridge University Press, New York

www.cambridge.org
Information on this title: www.cambridge.org/9780521140034

First published 2011

Cover design by Jenny Cowan.
Typeset by Aptara Corp.
Printed in Australia by Ligare Pty Ltd.

*A catalogue record for this publication is available from the British Library*

*National Library of Australia Cataloguing in Publication data*
  Glover, Dennis.
  The art of great speeches : and why we remember them / Dennis Glover.
  9780521140034 (pbk.)
  Includes bibliographical references and index.
  Speeches, addresses, etc.
808.85

ISBN 978-0-521-14003-4 Paperback

# Contents

# Speeches

# Photographs

# Acknowledgements

Special thanks to Tony Moore from Cambridge University Press (CUP), and Dominic Grounds for encouraging me to write the book; Stephen Hepburn of Coventry Bookstore for convincing me there was a market for it; Debbie Lee, Susan Hanley and Jodie Howell from CUP for making it happen; Helen Bethune Moore for editing the manuscript; Fiona Hehir for compiling the index; local café proprietors for providing a place to write it; my many former employers and clients for giving me the opportunity to learn my trade the hard way; and my fellow speechwriters and political associates for the insights and ideas that they have provided over the years.

Grateful acknowledgement is made to the following publishers for permission to reproduce extracts from previously published material. Penguin: *The Civil Wars*, Appian, trans. John Carter, 1996; *The Makers of Rome*, Plutarch, trans. Ian Scott-Kilvert, 1965; *Selected Works*, Cicero, trans. Michael Grant, 1971; *The Greek Sophists*, trans., introduction and notes John Dillon and Tania Gergel; *On Government*, Cicero, trans. Michael Grant, 1993; *The Coming of the Third Reich*, Richard Evans, 2003; *Lysistrata and Other Plays*, Aristophanes, trans. and introduction by Alan H. Sommerstein, 2002; Yale University Press; *Five Days in London: May 1940*, John Lukacs, 1999.

Every effort has been made to trace and acknowledge copyright. The publisher apologises for any accidental infringement and welcomes information that would redress this situation.

# Introduction

## 1

❧ ❧ ❧

A few years ago in my country there was a minor media storm. Newspapers began reporting the 'scandal' that some politicians had been hiring a speechwriter to draft their speeches. It became an issue on talkback radio; the speechwriter became a target of anger, and it culminated in headlines like: 'Another minister caught using a speechwriter'. That speechwriter was me.

This episode struck me as strange. After all, isn't making speeches what politicians are supposed to do? Aren't the politicians we love the most the ones who employ the best speechwriters? Isn't it the case that words can outlive deeds and inspire the best to run for office? What, after all, are the Kennedys and Martin Luther King today but a rich legacy of inspiration for a new generation? And don't the newspapers usually applaud loudly when a politician makes a speech that's intelligent, witty, surprising and inspiring? Those headlines seemed to me the equivalent of: 'surgeon caught buying sharper scalpel'.

Some time later, the same newspapers had another complaint: the dismal standard of oratory of modern politicians, especially the then Australian prime minister Kevin Rudd, who in one prominent editorial was given '10 out of 10 for content, nought out of ten for delivery'. This happened in the United States and Britain too, where Republican presidential nominee John McCain was overshadowed by his own previously unknown running mate, and Gordon Brown was commonly voted the most boring public speaker in the nation – more boring even than the notoriously inarticulate football player David Beckham. This is a major problem: the inability to articulate a sense of purpose and direction and inspire others to follow can drain leaders, parties and governments of energy and support, and cause much needed reform to fail. Why is it happening?

The answer, in part, is 'too much information'. Politicians today seem in thrall to contestable facts. Every generation is dominated by certain professions – our parents' by engineers and sociologists; ours by economists and pollsters. The effect has been to turn our elected representatives from leaders into technocrats. Afraid of being accused of sounding inauthentic or lightweight, or off-message, or spouting rhetoric, their words and eventually their own personalities become pre-programmed and predictable. Their speech drowns in their numbers and economic modelling. It's a failing compounded by a political backroom culture that makes it easy to get to the top without ever having mastered the art of oratory. Common to both left and right, this failing is robbing our democracy of energy, and the cost is paid in the wreckage of governments and political movements unable to enthuse their followers or provide an adequate riposte to their opponents. In Australia, even the hardest heads in the national press gallery agreed that Kevin Rudd's poor oratory contributed to his dramatic downfall and replacement as prime minister by the more engaging Julia Gillard.

This failure of the good to inspire too often leaves us with an invidious choice – between the dour and the demagogue. The choice should be unnecessary.

## 2

Why is there resistance today to good speechwriting and good oratory, especially when the appearance of a great speechmaker is always greeted with extraordinary public enthusiasm? Whenever a new one appears you can almost see the electorate bending towards the stage, eager for more.

The arguments against putting real effort into oratory – including the arguments against hiring speechwriters, once directed against me – come down to this: our politicians should always speak to us plainly, without artifice, and especially without their words being written by others. This seems common sense, and, in a naïve way, even idealistic. But in an age when politicians commonly make two or three speeches in a single day, as well as actually run the country, is it practical to ask them to research and write them all themselves? More importantly, is it desirable?

This question may sound like special pleading from someone who makes his living by writing speeches for others, but it is in fact a question almost as old as democracy itself.

In 161 BC the Roman Senate decided that anyone caught writing speeches for others faced expulsion from the city. The senators were acting on a belief that originated in a famous philosophical debate some 250 years prior between members of the Platonic Academy and their rivals the Sophists. The former believed that political decisions should be based on the truth alone, guided by the advice of the best philosophers. The employment of experts to advise in the arts of persuasion, they reasoned, would potentially make 'the weaker argument the stronger' – something dangerous in the Athens of their day when matters of life and death were decided by majority vote in mass citizen assemblies. The latter, the Sophists, disagreed. More politically realistic, they recognised something we can all observe today: when it comes to politics, humans are swayed by emotion as much as by logic and facts.

As taxpayers, mortgage holders, shareholders and political advisers, we all have an interest in the logical presentation of facts, especially numbers with dollar signs attached to them. Presenting facts logically is an important part of successful political speechmaking. But as humans we need more. For good or ill, our minds respond to emotional stimulation. There's much more to our lives than the things we can count. The very existence of religion, for instance, shows that we want so much more: spiritual uplift, moral affirmation, inspiration, a quest. Our politicians need to give us these things; if they don't they are neglecting one-half of our brains and one-half of their job.

This observation is so obvious to most people that it hardly seems worth mentioning, but still so many politicians continue to ignore it. Armed with consultancy reports as thick as telephone books and PowerPoint slide decks of increasing sophistication, they think the rational exposition of the facts alone will defeat the enemies of thoughtful progress or considered conservatism. And they are egged on by the (usually well-scripted and highly emotive) proponents of 'plain talking' and 'common sense' who dominate the airwaves and denounce the arts of persuasion as the spin practised by hollow apparatchiks. We are, it seems, in Athens once more, where the knowledgeable and the good are condemned to eternal defeat by the shallow and the bad.

Is there a way out?

The answer comes from Rome. In the first century BC, Rome witnessed a revival of classical rhetoric. As the increasingly anarchic republic, weakened by the assaults of populist demagogues, began to fall apart, the foremost orator and thinker of the day, Cicero, recognised that the defenders of the republic could only prevail if they first shed their moral qualms about appealing to the masses. He recognised that in the world in which we actually live, as opposed to the world that exists in the clouds sometimes inhabited by philosophers, the good may choose to ignore the arts of persuasion, but the bad certainly will not. Cicero believed his troubled times were ones for good people to wise up about the realities of popular opinion: that it was fickle, responsive to emotional stimulus, and could be won over by eloquence. The most knowledgeable and just people, he argued, had an obligation not just to be to smart and true, but also to become effective orators. Cicero's message was that persuasion need not mean hollow, cynical, confected spin; it can mean endowing truth, judgement and moral integrity with greater force.

**3**

This book is dedicated to Cicero's ideal. It addresses a question posed by a despairing newspaper commentator:

How can intelligent, democratic politics survive when the best lack conviction and the worst monopolise passion? What hope for the civilising activity of politics when convictions are constantly trimmed and abandoned to meet the demands of the modern world's high-velocity media?

I come from the liberal or progressive side of politics, but my many conservative friends share the same concerns. So whether you are left or right, if you are worried about the threat to democratic politics posed by the screaming pedlars of cynicism and dishonesty, or equally concerned about the triumph of shallowness over substance, you have a duty to put your case more persuasively. This book aims to help.

It can be read in a number of ways:

- As the foregoing suggests, as a defence of oratory – with its potential to unite passion with substance and ethics in the name of democracy – against its detractors
- As a history of oratory and an attempt to understand how it has evolved – from classical times, via the genius of Renaissance writers such as Shakespeare, to the digital age
- As explanation of how oratory works – uncovering the simple components of the art of rhetoric to enable those accepting the noble call of public life to speak more effectively, and to arm the rest of us, plain citizens, with the ability to recognise when persuasion stops and demagoguery begins
- As a source of technical and practical lessons for the budding speechwriter.

As in any endeavour, it helps to examine success. The book therefore uses the insights provided by the classical authorities, notably Cicero himself, to analyse the great speeches in history. Bookshop shelves bend under the weight of collections of 'great', 'stirring', 'history-changing' speeches, but few explain how those speeches work and why they deserve those adjectives. Here, we break down the speeches we all know – by Socrates, Shakespeare's most memorable orators, Winston Churchill, the Kennedys, Martin Luther King and many others, including characters from TV series like *The West Wing*, popular movies and novels – to show how their speechwriters connect with audiences, seize the moment, appeal to emotions, project the speaker's character, use facts convincingly and destroy their opponents' arguments to try to force the hand of history or create memorable drama.

Along the way I add some humble examples from my own speechwriting experience on the staff of political leaders to demonstrate how the lessons from the masters can be applied in practice.

In chapter 1 our story is bookended by two passionate debates: between Marcus Brutus and Mark Antony following the assassination of Julius Caesar in 44 BC, and between Barack Obama or Sarah Palin in the US presidential campaign of 2008. Depending on your politics you will likely love or loathe Obama or Palin, but what no one can deny is their quality as orators. As we shall see throughout the book, the reason for this is that, in large part, they and their speechwriters follow the rules set out by the classical authorities.

The elements of classical and modern oratory are then discussed in chapters 3 to 7 – 'moment', style, emotion, character and evidence.

In chapter 8 we discuss the morality of speech and why writing and delivering great speeches is so important.

Then in chapter 9 we see how these elements of the DNA of oratory bring to life the most famous and influential speech of the modern era, the Gettysburg Address.

In chapter 10, drawing on my own experiences and those of the great contemporary speechwriters, we examine how speeches are written and how speechwriters are made.

We then conclude by considering who in the modern era can be regarded as Cicero's ideal orator.

Doubtless many will argue that I have neglected *their* favourite great speech. Everyone will have a slightly different list, but it's my hope that the analysis provided here enables everyone to look again at his or her favourite oration and understand why it is so gripping, why it works.

The book is aimed at everyday people in their duties as citizens. It avoids academic controversies, not because it considers them trivial, but because, in the spirit of Cicero himself, I believe that significant ideas, especially those of practical political importance, can and must be grasped by everyone if our democracies are to survive and flourish.

Our story about oratory starts, as so many do, in the classical world.

# Chapter 1
## To save a republic

### 1

───────────── ❧ ❧ ❧ ─────────────

15 March 44 BC began tensely. Some four weeks before, the Senate, menaced by threatening mobs, had appointed the populist general Julius Caesar dictator for life. Now, in every place where people gathered – bath houses, market places, temples – the speculation was intense. Was this the end of the Republic that had lasted for more than four-and-a-half centuries? Would anyone stand up to save it and the liberties it guaranteed? Talk of assassination was common, but Caesar, scorning precautions, dismissed his guard and travelled in a simple litter to that day's scheduled meeting of the Senate in the Forum Romanum – a vast, rectangular meeting place, 200 metres long and 75 wide, bordered lengthwise by up-market shops and apartments, and endwise by government offices. At the northern end, dominated by a steep cliff leading to the Capitol Hill, stood the Tabularium (national archive); the Temple of Saturn (state treasury); the Temple of Concord; and the new Senate House (the old having been burnt down by rioting supporters of the murdered demagogue Publius Clodius eight years before). In

The Forum Romanum – the original speakers' forum, looking down from the Capitol where Brutus proclaimed liberty (the Rostra would have been middle left of the photograph). Photo: © F.C.G./Shutterstock.com.

front of the Senate House lay the Comitium, the political assembly ground where senators addressed citizens from the Rostra, the raised speaking platform made from the wooden prows of captured warships. Opposite, at the southern end of the Forum lay the Temple of Castor and Pollux, from which the tribunes addressed rowdy gatherings of the plebs, watched over by the club-wielding thugs of the city's various factions.

Caesar's view of Rome's heart would have been rather different to the one we are used to seeing in Hollywood movies; it was still ramshackle and brick, not yet replaced by the marble caricature of sham democracy that plutocracies prefer; Ridley Scott's computer-generated imperial city had yet to be built. The Forum – the epicentre of the Roman state – was still, above all else, a place dedicated to political speech. Riot, murder and factional mobs may have made it dangerous to enter, but in this arena the essence of classical democracy – persuasion – still had the potential to carry the day and, just possibly, change the future course of history, as Caesar's fatal entry to the Senate chamber was about to prove.

Stopped on his path to his ceremonial chair by Tillius Cimber, Caesar was hacked to death by some 60 aristocratic conspirators, 'falling', according to the historian Appian, 'neatly' at the foot of Pompey's statue. As the blood spread across the marble floor, the astonished senators, Rome, the world, held their breath.

Caesar's power had rested on money and violence. Now that he was dead the vacuum was to be filled by a more legitimate source of Roman power – oratory. Over the following three days in the Forum Romans witnessed an extraordinary rhetorical duel between deadly enemies: the assassins led by Marcus Junius Brutus, who wanted to re-establish a true republic; and the crude but effective master of horse, Mark Antony, who wanted to assume the dead dictator's powers.

It all started rather unheroically. Blood drenched and adrenalin charged after the killing, Brutus turned to the terrified senators standing astonished in the chamber and urged them to grasp their recovered freedom. But they fled and were joined by a panicked crowd rushing from games in the adjacent Theatre of Pompey. One can imagine the equivalent effect if a president or prime minister were to be gunned down outside a packed Super Bowl or an FA Cup Final. Undeterred, the conspirators rushed to the steps of the Capitol where, according to Plutarch, Brutus, brandishing his dagger over his head, proclaimed liberty. As the panic subsided and a crowd assembled, Brutus made a speech 'calculated to suit the occasion' and was applauded strongly, then urged to go down to the Rostra to address the city. There, Brutus spoke again, but his reassuring oratory was undone by the praetor Lucius Cornelius Cinna, who, misjudging the mood, violently denounced Caesar and was howled down. The assassins were then chased back up the hill, where they barricaded themselves into public buildings to think again.

Two days of tense negotiations followed.

But on the 17th the Senate finally met. In a state of extraordinary tension it debated and passed a compromise motion that neither condemned the assassins nor declared

Caesar a tyrant, but granted a general amnesty to all sides, and divided command of the Empire between the leading players.

But it was a fudge – one which the citizens in the Forum were about to settle with consequences that were to last centuries.

When the Senate rose, Brutus called the people up to the steps of the Capitol once more and urged them to enjoy their newly found state of freedom, repudiate the oaths of fidelity that had made them vassals to Caesar, and accept the tyrannicide as lawful. 'Romans,' he said, would rather 'die a thousand times rather than consent under oath to serve as slaves.' But he knew that democratic rhetoric wasn't sufficient, and wisely reassured all that the grants of land Caesar had recently made to them would stand. Momentarily, Brutus' oratory had swayed the people to the conspirators' side. The day, however, wasn't over.

Later, after the proclamation of the Senate's amnesty decrees, and hostages had been exchanged, Brutus' party was invited down to the Forum where it was clapped and cheered. The crowd's mood, however, suddenly changed. Antony had earlier convinced the senators to give Caesar public funeral rites and to publicly disclose his will, which had been generous to the plebs. The reading of the will, followed by the dramatic delivery of Caesar's body by a large and aggressive retinue, turned the crowd's sympathies the other way. This was where the fate of the Republic would be decided. Antony stepped up to the Rostra and, recalling Caesar's nobility and love for the people, reminded the audience of their oath to defend Caesar. The people were roused to a white-hot fury. The historian Appian gives us a sense of the mesmerising theatricality of Antony's address:

> In this inspired frenzy he said much else, altering his voice from clarion-clear to dirge-like, grieving for Caesar as for a friend who had suffered injustice, weeping and vowing that he desired to give his life for Caesar's. Then, swept very easily on to passionate emotion, he stripped the clothes

from Caesar's body, raised them on a pole and waved them about, rent as they were by the stabs and befouled with the dictator's blood. At this the people, like a chorus, joined him in the most sorrowful lamentation and after this expression of emotion were again filled with anger.

Plutarch's account describes the speech's destructive impact on its audience:

> As soon as he saw that the people were deeply stirred by his speech, he changed his tone and struck a note of compassion, and picking up Caesar's robe, stiff with blood as it was, he unfolded it for all to see, pointing out each gash where the daggers had stabbed through and the number of Caesar's wounds. At this the audience lost all control of their emotions. Some shouted aloud to kill the murderers, others, as had happened in the riot in which Clodius the demagogue had lost his life, dragged out benches and tables from neighbouring shops and piled them on top of one another to make an enormous pyre. On this they laid Caesar's corpse and set fire to it ... Then, as the flames began to mount, people rushed up from all sides, seized burning brands, and ran through the city to the murderers' houses to set them alight.

The dogs of war having been set loose by wild oratory, Brutus' party wisely slipped out of the city. Liberty and republicanism collapsed, exhausted, into a long and deep sleep – in which state they remained until reawakened by the popular rediscovery of classical rhetoric fifteen centuries later.

## 2

Most know of this story through its dramatic rendering in Act 3, Scene 2 of Shakespeare's *Julius Caesar*. In the play the action and oratory are necessarily compressed, moving directly from the

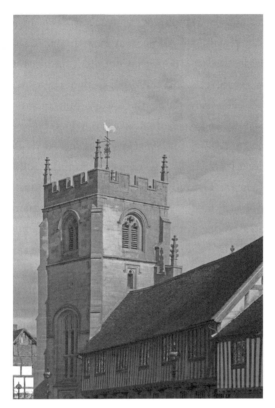

Stratford Guild School – school of classical rhetoric if not of classical architecture. Photo: © David Hughes/Shutterstock.com.

assassination to the Forum and the decisive debate. But while Shakespeare's account may be inaccurate history, it provides rich insights into the sort of oratory that the original Romans would have employed. There's a simple reason for this: its author was not just one of the finest dramatists to ever pick up a pen; he also wrote in an age when a person's education was judged above all on their command of classical rhetoric – the basis of oratory – and in this respect Shakespeare's education was first class.

As any lover of literature knows, William Shakespeare received his formal education in the Stratford Guild School, which still stands. With its Tudor construction of warped wooden beams and roughly rendered brick it looks anything but classical; there wasn't and still isn't a single Doric column in sight. Hardly the surroundings, one would think, to teach a deep appreciation of the politics of republican Rome. But as with any school, it's what went on inside the classroom that counted, and in Shakespeare's classroom one subject stood supreme: Roman rhetoric.

By the middle of the sixteenth century, humanism – the revival of classical Greek and Roman knowledge, which had begun in Florence 150 years before – had transformed the curriculum of even the humblest of England's 360 or more grammar schools, including Shakespeare's. The movement's goal was to equip citizens and especially political leaders with the cultural attainments necessary for the continuation of a well-governed society – something they believed could only be done through the study of the *studia humanitatis*: grammar, rhetoric, poetry, history and moral philosophy.

The syllabus Shakespeare faced would have stretched students of any age, making the most exacting twenty-first century enforcers of standards look positively lowbrow. His list of required authors would have appeared ominous indeed: Ovid, Virgil, Horace, Caesar, Cicero, Quintilian, and their modern commentators Erasmus, Susenbrotus and others.

Shakespeare's schooling would have been neither lightweight nor light-hearted. Here's how a renowned Shakespeare scholar describes it:

In the summer the school day began at 6 a.m.; in the winter, as a concession to the darkness and the cold, at 7. At 11 came recess for lunch – Will presumably ran home, only three hundred yards or so away – and then instruction began again, continuing until 5:30 or 6. Six days a week; twelve months a year. The curriculum made few concessions to the range of human interests: no English history or literature; no biology, chemistry, or physics; no economics or sociology; only a smattering of arithmetic. There was instruction in the articles of the Christian faith, but that must have seemed all but indistinguishable from the instruction in Latin. And the instruction was not gentle: rote memorization, relentless drills, endless repetition, daily analysis of texts, elaborate exercises in imitation and rhetorical variation, all backed up by the threat of violence.

But at the end of each day, if he could stay attentive, young Will would have learnt a great deal indeed. Students were expected to make significant progress each year towards the ideal of an educated man (and women in cases like Elizabeth I). One of the most prominent Elizabethan educational theorists, William Kempe, set out what was expected in each year of schooling:

- first form – learning by heart the parts of Latin speech, including the declension of nouns and the conjugation of verbs
- second form – practice the precepts of grammar through study of Latin authors
- third form – reading moderately difficult texts like Cicero's letters
- fourth and fifth form – making translations
- sixth form – Latin composition, participation in mock debates speaking first *pro* and then *contra*, and, for the truly gifted, learning Greek.

Once described by Ben Johnson as having 'small Latin and less Greek', it's possible Shakespeare may not have had a gift for foreign languages. But it's almost impossible that, having survived this ordeal by rote learning, during which he would have been drilled relentlessly on the components of the Latin language and the techniques of its use in oratory, he would not have emerged formidably armed to re-imagine the speechmaking that occurred in the Roman Forum following the assassination of Julius Caesar.

In fact Shakespeare had access to the very same sources we rely upon today as we try to understand exactly what was said (or at least *how* it was said) on the Ides of March, namely Thomas North's translation of Plutarch, and William Barker's translation of Appian. And unless new excavations turn up some unknown and long-lost verbatim transcripts by Tiro (Cicero's personal secretary and putative inventor of shorthand), Shakespeare's account is likely to be as close as we will get to an understanding of what the debate was like.

Brutus' defence of the tyrannicide – that it returned to Romans their liberty – is summed up in his neat question that appeals to the audience's noble sentiments:

> Had you rather Caesar were living and die all slaves, than
> that Caesar were dead, to live all free men?

The speech, like this fragment, is formidably eloquent. But – as we will examine in chapters that follow – it was perhaps too eloquent. One suspects that Shakespeare was having a little fun, ladling on the unsubtle rhetorical constructions and high-minded appeals in a way his fellow survivors of mock school debates would have remembered. His Brutus is just too poetic and too good to win the total respect of the unwashed plebs assembled beneath the Rostra. Shakespeare makes him a recognisable figure to those familiar with the Tony Benns and Teddy Kennedys of recent years: the noble and honourable gentleman radical; the inheritor of the family's political business; the earnest reformer given to speaking of equality in elevated tones to those without country houses and varnished yachts. Perfect, one would have thought, for a solid English actor like James Mason in the 1953 Hollywood adaptation of *Julius Caesar* by Joseph L. Mankiewicz.

Following the classical authorities, Shakespeare gives Antony a far more populist edge. Here is that other familiar modern political figure: the demagogue who speaks the language of the people better than any liberal silvertail ever could, but whose aim is to ride on their backs to wealth and power. The speech is classical, although not in the way Brutus' is – where style is employed to attract the ear. Its classicism lies in its blunt employment of redescription (or what we might today call 'doublespeak') to disguise Antony's ulterior motives, such as the subtle dissimulation summed up in Antony's claim that:

Brutus, gentleman orator – James Mason gets acting tips from director Joseph L. Mankiewicz. Photo: © Time & Life Pictures/Getty Images.

I come to bury Caesar, not to praise him.

It also lies in its artful exploitation of the audience's emotions and greed, as when Antony feigns withholding Caesar's will to the audience, saying:

'Tis good you know not that you are his heirs; for, if you
should, O, what would come of it!

The contrast with Brutus couldn't be more stark: the mismatch between words and ends, the eloquent denials of eloquence, the cunning manipulation of the audience's self-interest, and the theatrical arousal of its base emotions. And who else would Mankiewicz turn to, but the actor who was passion personified? Marlon Brando.

We know how this movie ends: with the audience, against Antony's stated intention, turning the Forum into Caesar's funeral

Antony, passionate, crude, effective – 'the most unkindest cut of all'.
Photo: © Time & Life Pictures/Getty Images.

pyre and setting out with flaming torches to hunt down the traitors who murdered him. Antony's oratory wins the day.

Shakespeare had grasped an important truth from his lessons: when it comes to political oratory, reason, charm and poetic eloquence may be important, but unless that oratory can rouse the passions, it will lose out to demagoguery every time.

# 3

In the modern United States, communications technologies have made the political forum nationwide. Through radio, television and the internet Americans can now hear, see and read their politicians' speeches even if they can't physically stand beneath the rostra. In fact, it's safe to assume American political debates are followed by a far higher proportion of Americans than Roman debates were followed by Romans – especially in 2008.

The week straddling the end of August and the beginning of September 2008 was one of the most highly charged in recent US politics. Seldom would the Republic's debates have been so closely followed. Around the office water cooler, at the local bar or drug store, in a cab – anywhere Americans could gather together and talk, watch television, use the internet or listen to talk radio – one topic dominated all others: the presidential election and that week's nominating conventions. Few such election campaigns had been so anticipated or had provoked such partisan passions. The nation was engaged in two simultaneous wars, neither of which were going well. Its economy was in deep recession, beginning to feel underfoot the strengthening tremors of a global financial crisis that was about to bring its banking system crashing down within just six weeks. And its culture had been split by a two-decade-long ideological war between the liberal left and the conservative right. Into this potentially revolutionary situation stepped two of the most polarising candidates imaginable: the liberal presumptive Democratic nominee Barack Obama, and John McCain's presumptive Republican vice-presidential running mate and cherished child of the neo-conservative counter-revolution, Sarah Palin.

Oratory had not played much of a role in recent American elections. In fact the speech itself had been in decline for some decades: reduced by the format of the nightly television news bulletin into 'the grab' and 'the sound bite'; dismissed by talkback demagogues as the dishonest device of silky-tongued elites; and rejected by progressive opinion pollsters as inferior in effect to the triangulated message and the television ad buy. Eloquence, it seemed, was the tool of the naïve. It was passé, old school, last century. Barack Obama and Sarah Palin were about to change all that.

Within four years Obama had risen from being an obscure Illinois state legislator to a viable contender for the most powerful office in the world for one major reason: he could speak like few others. Obama had announced himself to the world at the previous Democratic convention with an acclaimed address framed around the Latin rhetoric on the official seal of the United States,

*E pluribus unum* ('out of many, one'). The speech contained a formulation guaranteed to appeal to a Democratic Party which at that time seemed incapable of countering the Republican charge that it was too liberal, too elite, too secular and insufficiently patriotic:

> There's not a liberal America and a conservative America –
> there's the United States of America. There's not a black
> America and white America and Latino America and Asian
> America – there's the United States of America . . . The
> pundits like to slice-and-dice our country into Red States
> and Blue States; Red States for Republicans, Blue States for
> Democrats. But I've got news for them, too. We worship an
> "awesome God" in the Blue States, and we don't like federal
> agents poking around our libraries in the Red States. We
> coach Little League in the Blue States and yes, we've got
> some gay friends in the Red States. There are patriots who
> opposed the war in Iraq and patriots who supported the war
> in Iraq. We are one people, all of us pledging allegiance to
> the stars and stripes, all of us defending the United States of
> America.

Eloquence also helped him dispatch his rival for the Democratic nomination, Hillary Rodham Clinton, whose triangulating, message-driven appearances seemed somehow enervating and calculating alongside the lofty and idealistic speeches Obama made to rapt, cheering crowds.

He had to be matched, and in Sarah Palin the Republican strategists were confident they had someone just as capable on her feet and capable of mobilising their party's base. It was as if, with so much at stake, and such a stark choice to be made, the electorate had instinctively been drawn back to the essence and originating force of democratic politics: oratory

The convention organisers seemed to be aware of this tide taking people back to the Roman Forum – in Obama's case, literally so.

On 28 August 2008, at 5:15 p.m., some three hours before he was due to speak, almost 80 000 Democratic supporters and

Hillary Rodham Clinton – triangulation, not inspiration. Photo: © Jose
Gil/Shutterstock.com.

members of the media had packed into the Denver Broncos' stadium, Invesco Field, to see the playing surface covered by a modern
interpretation of the Forum Romanum – at its centre a raised rostra, partly encircled by Doric columns. If Ridley Scott's computer
technicians were called upon to recreate the sight at the steps of
the Capitol from which Brutus spoke in 44 BC, this is what, with
Hollywood licence, we could probably expect.

The staging had its desired effect. The *New York Times* reported
the speech had been watched by at least 40 million viewers, making
it the most watched convention speech ever, thanks in part to the
television-friendly classically inspired stage set, which couldn't have
worked better.

Invesco Field – twenty-first century Forum Romanum. Photo: © Getty Images.

It is also difficult to know how the oratory – which, like Brutus' and Antony's, we will analyse later – could have been better.

Obama's task had been that of every political orator: to turn the situation to his advantage. Had a modern Appian turned his mind to report it, he would have put Obama's success at the convention down to three factors:

1 Overcoming, at last, the Republicans' long-successful strategy of marginalising the Democrats as an elite, unpatriotic, celebrity-fixated minority, secretly contemptuous of ordinary people (a considerable feat given Obama's back story as a Harvard-educated African-American who had never served in the armed forces).

> I don't know what kind of lives John McCain thinks that celebrities [like me] lead, but this has been mine . . .

2 Turning the anger of those ordinary people over recent economic and military failure into rage against the incumbent Republicans.

> In Washington they call this [Republican
> trickle-down economics] the 'Ownership Society',
> but what it really means is that you're on your
> own . . .

3  Not allowing his opponent McCain to distance himself from
   the failures of his party.

> John McCain likes to say that he'll follow bin Laden
> to the gates of hell, but he won't even follow him to
> the cave where he lives.

A modern-day Plutarch would have observed that such was
Obama's command of his audience's passions that for many this
night would be remembered as one of the greatest of their lives,
and one that confirmed them in their life's choice to be liberal
idealists. For many it would have been bettered only by his victory
speech on election night itself.

Sarah Palin's speech a week later on 3 September, watched
by an equally record-breaking television audience, did not try to
create a similar Roman backdrop, but it isn't difficult to see in the
stadiums in which conventions are held, packed with chanting, die-
hard supporters, the attempt to recreate the pulsing atmosphere of
Roman republican political meetings.

And pulse is what she provided in a witty, at times spontaneous, but thoroughly calculated address that played to her supporters' deepest convictions and contained devastating ridicule of
her Democratic opponents.

Sarah Palin's speech had different objectives:

1  To introduce herself to the voters.

> I had the privilege of living most of my life in a small
> town. I was just your average hockey mom and
> signed up for the PTA. I love those hockey moms.
> You know, they say the difference between a hockey
> mom and a pit bull? Lipstick.

Sarah Palin hits it out of the park. Photo: © mistydawnphoto/
Shutterstock.com.

2   To turn Barak Obama's rhetorical strengths into weaknesses
    through mockery.

> Listening to him speak, it's easy to forget that this is
> a man who has authored two memoirs but not a
> single major law or even a reform, not even in the
> State Senate.

As even Palin's liberal opponents conceded, she didn't just succeed,
she hit it out of the park, and by the end of that night many Republicans were left wishing that she, not McCain, was their party's
presidential nominee.

But while these speeches and those by Brutus and Antony had
differing objectives, reading them alerts us to many similarities:

their attempts to establish rapport with the common people; their appeals to patriotism; the repeated establishment of contrasts between speakers and their opponents; their claims to be speaking plainly, without recourse to dishonest rhetorical devices; the use of stories to establish the speakers' characters, and the use of devices that catch the ear, such as repetition, alliteration and poetic rhythm. These similarities were no coincidence. The participants in these rhetorical duels may have been some 20 centuries apart, but time is really all that separates them. Linking them, via the genius of William Shakespeare and his contemporaries, was a man whose most important legacy was to lay the foundations for the modern world's understanding of the nature and importance of political oratory. His name was Marcus Tullius Cicero – and, coincidentally enough, he just happened to be an eyewitness to the assassination of Julius Caesar.

# 4

~~~ ❧ ❧ ❧ ~~~

When Brutus, splattered with Caesar's warm blood, turned to face the astonished senators assembled in the room before his fellow assassins, his very first act was to call out to Cicero. Brutus congratulated him on the recovery of his liberty and urged him to convince the Senate to endorse the tyrannicide and restore the Republic. Why Cicero? This man, Cicero, was no ordinary senator. A former consul – the equivalent today of a former prime minister or president – he was the most articulate spokesman for the republican and senatorial cause, the greatest orator of his day, and (if his own immodest claims are to be believed) perhaps of all time.

> O fortunatam natam me consule Romam.
> O happy Rome, born in my consulship!

Cicero had only minor involvement in the assassination. He had been left out of the conspiracy itself due to what today would be put down to character issues: he was regarded as lacking resolution and discretion – a judgement confirmed only when he ignored Brutus and other importuning assassins and joined the herd of Senators fleeing from the scene of the stabbing. They were crying out for good reason. Cicero's seniority and public respect made his endorsement vital to the conspiracy's longer-term success. But more immediately, the conspirators knew that his voice (in the most literal sense) could be decisive.

Cicero – the ideal orator. Photo: © Jozef Sedmak/Shutterstock.com.

Despite running to his Palatine Hill mansion somewhere past the far end of the Forum (a show-off property he had picked up for 3.5 million sesterces some years before with his earnings as the priciest criminal barrister of his day), Cicero was overjoyed at the news of the assassination. It was no wonder, because Caesar's dictatorship and the years of triumviral rule that preceded it had rendered worthless the one quality that it had been his life's work to perfect: oratory.

Born on 3 January 106 BC in the town of Arpinum, Cicero was neither from Rome nor the son of one of its great senatorial families. This was to prove our benefit, because as a new man, or *novus homus*, he was forced to seek glory the hard way, and in Rome that meant obtaining eloquence.

Fortunately for Cicero, his father was wealthy enough to give him the best education money could buy, and he, his brother and two cousins were placed under the personal tutorship of the leading philosophers and rhetoricians at Rome and Athens – a grounding Cicero completed by taking himself to study philosophy under the famous stoic Posidonius at Rhodes, law under the renowned jurists the Scaevolae in Rome, and politics under the exiled statesman Publius Rutilius Rufus at Smyrna. The equivalent today would be, say, a BA from Oxford (a starred first of course), followed by postgraduate study under a succession of Nobel Prize-winning professors at Cambridge, Princeton and Harvard.

By his mid-30s, Cicero had gained a complete mastery of the art of rhetoric, and in a famous case against the murdering and extorting provincial governor Gaius Verres, had triumphed to supplant Quintus Hortensius Hortalus as the leading jurist of his day. Then, by way of minor offices and by ingratiating himself with the spectacularly wealthy general-statesman Pompey the Great, he rose to consul in 63 BC, and during his two-year term uncovered a supposed conspiracy of Lucius Catilina (Catiline) to overthrow the Republic – a victory he never let anyone forget but which also created bitter enemies who would later check his career. 'Thanks to a combination of his vanity, his gift for self-invention and the diligence of his secretary Tiro, some 58 speeches by Cicero have survived to this day out of an estimated total of 88 major speeches he made.' But the days when oratory could hold the faction-riddled Republic together were numbered.

In 60 BC the three most powerful men in Rome – Pompey, Crassus and Caesar – reached a truce, agreeing to divide up control of the state and its empire among themselves. With the independence of the courts and the Senate effectively destroyed, Cicero's oratory had lost its power. As he later put it, with typical eloquence:

The voice of Hortensius was silenced only by his own death; mine by the death of the Republic.

After a period of exile, Cicero decided in 55 BC to retreat to his villa in Tusculum to write, returning to Rome only to take up various duties as necessity demanded. Over the following decade – which included the period of Caesar's rule from 49 BC to his assassination in 44 BC – Cicero produced a body of written work that was to have a major impact on the European Renaissance fifteen centuries later and in the half-dozen centuries since.

Inevitably, this meant writing about oratory. Six major works on the subject survive. Equally inevitably perhaps, it meant writing about himself. But interestingly for our story, two other men featured in Cicero's writings even more than Cicero: Brutus and Antony.

In his writings on oratory, Cicero did a number of things. He laid out, following accepted – largely Greek – conventions, a set of technical treatises on effective oratory:

- the various categories of speeches that can be identified
- how they can be composed and delivered most effectively
- the subjects suitable to their use (these are discussed in chapter 2).

He also wrote a major history of oratory and the famous orators of Greece and Rome (not forgetting to imply that he – Cicero – was the greatest of them all).

And this exercise in vanity led to his third task: to define the ideal orator all should aspire to emulate. His formula was simple. Anyone could learn the techniques of oratory necessary to do a competent job, and those with a natural gift and willingness to practise hard could also do well; but truly great orators are extremely rare – rarer even than great generals – because the list of necessary accomplishments is so long. In an orator:

We demand the acuteness of a logician, the profundity of a philosopher, the diction virtually of a poet, the memory of a lawyer, the voice of a performer in tragic drama, the

gestures, you might also say, of an actor at the very top of
his profession.

But even these, narrowly defined, were not enough. Ultimately,
Cicero's ideal orator was someone who combined technical knowledge of a trade, natural talent and a capacity for hard work with
the qualities that can only be obtained through a liberal humanist
education: not just academic philosophical and legal knowledge but
also moral excellence, character, virtue, style and – above all else –
a love of reason, freedom and justice, and a willingness to serve
the state: 'a *vir bonus* and *vir civilis* – a good man possessing all the
virtues needed for civic life and whose virtues were amplified by
the possession of political office'.

The power of such an orator to improve the welfare of the
Republic was immense:

> His eloquence . . . gives him the power to throw culpable
> and guilty men to the wrath of their own fellow-
> countrymen: to suppress crime, by ensuring that it is
> punished. The protection his talent affords others can bring
> salvation to the innocent by rescuing them from
> condemnation in the courts. It is even in his capacity to
> transfigure a spiritless and misguided nation, to revive its
> sense of honour, to reclaim a whole people from its errors.
> He can stir up anger against evil men, or, when such anger
> has attacked innocent people, he can calm it down. Indeed
> his might as an orator will give him power to instil or
> eradicate within the hearts of mankind any and every
> passion that circumstances and occasions may demand.

Where was such a man, especially now, with the Republic crushed
by tyranny?

It was a crucial question, because Cicero understood that in the
absence of virtuous orators the political vacuum would be filled by
evil ones. Cicero's evidence was the damage caused by Tiberius and
Gaius Gracchus, the radical plebeian demagogues whose proposals

to redistribute Rome's wealth and political power a half a century before had so frightened the ruling classes that they invoked the ultimate law to have the brothers judicially murdered in the name of public safety. In his dialogue 'On the orator' Cicero had one of his speakers (and former teachers), Quintus Mucius Scaevola, describe the Gracchi as 'the best speakers he had ever heard but men whose ability to arouse the masses through oratory managed to bring the state to the brink of ruin'. In modern times the Gracchi's egalitarianism has an obvious social-democratic appeal, but to Cicero and his aristocratic colleagues the brothers' capacity to stir up opposition to the established order seemed much like that of Hitler to us. Oratory was too powerful a weapon to be left to such men.

A couple of virtuous orators had stood out from the pack: Lucius Licinius Crassus, a true rhetorical stylist, and the more laid back Marcus Antonius Orator, (perhaps not coincidentally the grandfather of Mark Antony). But there was another who was still alive and at the height of his powers: Marcus Junius Brutus. In 46 BC, as Cicero's despair over Caesar's rule deepened, he addressed two major treatises on oratory to Brutus, passing to him the baton as the supreme orator of Rome, and attempting to rouse him to use his voice to save the Republic from tyranny.

Cicero, though, had a bone to pick with Brutus first. While both lovers of the Republic, the two were on opposite sides of a topical debate over which form of oratory was best.

Brutus was a leading exponent of Atticism – an austere style that shunned rhetorical excess. Today we'd call it speaking plainly or speaking your mind without fancy words – delivering the message to a talkback radio audience perhaps, or presenting the focus-tested sound bites to the six o'clock news. It might use charm perhaps, but not passion. One thinks of Hillary Clinton or John McCain.

Cicero, by contrast, was the champion of the Asiatic style, which held that the best approach was the one best suited to the occasion and the audience. If the situation called for calmness and factuality, so be it, but if it called for slugging it out in the Forum with the likes of the Gracchi or the supporters of dictatorship, then the only response could be 'Bring it on'. In such circumstances the orator had a responsibility to use every rhetorical weapon to hand – poetic or guttural, logical or emotional, clean or dirty, whatever worked.

This was no dry academic dispute, because Cicero's experience had taught him that reason devoid of passion and guile was voiceless and prey to un-reason. Ultimately, he believed that by uniting reason and its partner wisdom with passionate eloquence and political hard-headedness, orators could save democracy from demagogues and in the process make it worth saving. This meant that saving the Republic would require good people to do more than put a calm and reasoned case – they would have to win over the Forum against all comers. The appeal to logic alone was bound to fail when the stakes were highest – including following the Ides of March. Cicero's aim was to rouse Brutus from his slumbers and send him suitably armed back to the Forum – now silenced by the dictatorship – to speak for Rome. The Forum, wrote Cicero, was Brutus' birthright, but now:

You are bereft of the republic and the republic of you.

As we have seen, Brutus, though brave, couldn't change his ways. The good remained too formal, too logical, too addicted to reason, too mindful of honour – strange virtues for those willing to kill – and ultimately ineffective. The Forum was left open to the Republic's ruthless enemies.

# 5

Cicero therefore decided to become the voice of Rome himself. If Brutus wouldn't do whatever it took, Rome's – the world's – supreme orator would.

Initially, as Antony's de facto dictatorship tightened its grip, Cicero followed the assassins out of the city, with the intention of going into permanent exile. Once again it seemed his nerve had failed him. But on the way to Greece, he stopped and turned around, re-entering Rome to lead the Republican resistance. With the majority of Rome's soldiers ultimately loyal to the memory of Caesar and the bribes his former deputy Antony and adoptive son Octavius could pay, oratory was one of the few weapons the Republicans had left.

Three days after his return Cicero delivered to the Senate and the Forum the first of 17 speeches which he dubbed 'the Philippics' after the Greek orator Demosthenes' famous attacks on Philip II of Macedonia more than three centuries before. Beginning in a conciliatory tone, these speeches – the second of which was circulated but never delivered – soon turned to deadly invective that denounced Antony as a morally degenerate traitor and called for his death. The stakes were high, because, should the resistance fail, the speeches marked Cicero for certain execution – just as Churchill's speeches had marked him for likely death had Hitler succeeded in invading Britain in 1940. With the stakes high, this, rather than the somewhat dodgy suppression of the Catiline conspiracy twenty years before, became Cicero's finest moment. A few excerpts from the second Philippic illustrate Cicero's willingness to mix passion with poetry when the circumstances required. Many of the characteristics of great speech are present: invective, storytelling, repetition and rhetorical questioning – but, most of all, idealism and courage:

> Would you like us to consider your behaviour from boyhood onwards Antony? I think so. Let us begin at the beginning. Your bankruptcy in early adolescence – do you remember that? Your father's fault, you will say. Certainly; and what a truly filial self-defence! . . . Then you graduated to man's clothing – or rather it was woman's as far as you were concerned. At first you were just a public prostitute, with a fixed price: quite a high one too. But very soon Curio intervened and took you off the streets, promoting you, one might say, to wifely status, and making a sound, steady,

married woman of you. No boy bought for sensual purposes was ever so completely in his master's power as you were in Curio's...

Senators, you are mourning three armies of Roman soldiers slain in battle: Antony killed them. You are sorrowing for great men of Rome: Antony robbed you of them. The authority of your order has been destroyed: Antony destroyed it. For every evil we have seen since that time [i.e., the civil war that began in 49 BC] – and what evils have we not seen? – he is responsible. There can be no other conclusion. He has been our Helen of Troy! He has brought upon our country war, pestilence and annihilation...

But let us leave the past. Your behaviour today, at the present day and moment at which I am speaking – defend that if you can! Explain why the Senate is surrounded by a ring of men with arms; why my listeners include gangsters of yours, sword in hand; why the doors of the Temple of Concord are closed; why you bring into the Forum the world's most savage people, Ituraeans, with their bows and arrows. I do these things in self-defence, says Antony. But surely a thousand deaths are better than the inability to live in one's own community without an armed guard...

your behaviour is a matter for yourself to decide. As for mine, I will declare how I shall conduct myself. When I was a young man I defended our state: in my old age I shall not abandon it. Having scorned the words of Catiline, I shall not be intimidated by yours. On the contrary, I would gladly offer my own body, if my death could redeem the freedom of my nation... Two things only I pray for. One, that in dying I may leave the Roman people free – the immortal gods could grant me no greater gift. My other prayer is this: that no man's fortunes may fail to correspond with his services to our country!

The threat to Antony's life in the last sentence was obvious, but it was past even Cicero's powers to defeat him. And when Antony formed an alliance with Octavian and forced the republican resistance to capitulate, he got his revenge, placing Cicero on the list of proscribed persons. Antony's henchmen caught up with Cicero as he fled once more, this time with even less conviction. And to acknowledge the vanquishing of Cicero's oratory, they cut off his head – which had uttered the Philippics – and his right hand – which had written them – and nailed them both to the Rostra in the Forum to act as a warning to others. The dictatorship preferred silence. The Republic, along with the free speech and oratory that had sustained it for four-and-a-half centuries, was gone. But a martyr to eloquence and free speech had been created.

# 6

Brutus, Antony, Shakespeare, Obama and Palin are linked by a golden thread more than two millennia long – the discovery in classical times of the potential political power that resides in the effective public use of language. As the next chapter will show, Cicero was by no means the first person to make this discovery. But thanks to his extraordinary eloquence and his vast corpus of surviving work, it was he, more than any other classical writer, who became the model of rhetorical and political virtuosity adopted by the writers and politicians of the Renaissance, who passed the tradition to us. We owe him a debt and a duty. Our next question is: just what secrets did Cicero and others uncover?

# Chapter 2

# Speech – the essence of democracy

## 1

Here is a sentence Cicero would have recognised, written by the man whose murder he celebrated:

> *Veni, vidi, vici.*
> I came, I saw, I conquered.

It proves that three little words are sometimes enough to convey the most profound thoughts. (And that they can be so much more elegant in Latin.)

Read it aloud a few times and you will notice some patterns. Why does it sound so appealing? What attracts the ear? Why is it remembered when so many of the author's other sentences are not?

Consider:

- each word starts with the same letter
- each ends with the same letter

- each has the same number of syllables
- it has three clauses
- if you rest the sentence on the apex of a triangle – between the *i* and *d* of *vidi* – it will balance
- it says pretty much all you need to know – or all its author wants you to know – about what happened
- it reflects well on the virtue of its subject.

The Greeks and Romans had technical terms for each of these rhetorical effects. They demonstrate something Cicero knew well: that certain ways of expressing yourself can attract an audience's attention more effectively and give our utterances greater force. But it is highly unlikely that the author was using them in a conscious fashion, ticking all the writer's stylistic and technical boxes, in the way that, say, Samuel Taylor Coleridge would have when he penned:

> In Xanadu did Kubla Khan
> A stately pleasure-dome decree:
> Where Alph, the sacred river, ran
> Through caverns measureless to man
> Down to a sunless sea.

It was written by a man of action, not a poet, boasting from the field about his conquest of Britain. And one can imagine how it was written – most likely hurriedly, dictated to a scribe between meetings of councils of war, or scribbled on a tablet over a makeshift desk piled high with military despatches of a far more urgent and consequential nature.

This demonstrates something else that Cicero also knew well: the prose use of rhetorical technique, even of the most poetic kind, is most usually a subconscious act. It would have come instinctively to the classically educated Caesar. This isn't unusual.

Even the greatest professional speechwriters produce their best work without thinking consciously about technique, much the way a great cellist plays Shostakovich's Concerto for Cello and Orchestra No. 1 in E-flat Major, Op. 107, without thinking too deeply about what his arms and hands are doing. It comes naturally. I once shared the stage of a literary festival with the doyen of Australian speechwriters, Graham Freudenberg, who wrote for the radical reforming Labor Prime Minister Gough Whitlam (Freudenberg should be thought of as the Australian equivalent of John F. Kennedy's speechwriter, Ted Sorensen). When I pointed out that the most remembered passages from his most celebrated speech (opposing Australia's commitment of troops to the Vietnam War, written for another Labor leader, Arthur Calwell),

> When the drums beat and the trumpets sound, the voice
> of reason and right can be heard in the land only with
> difficulty . . .

> I offer the probability that you will be traduced, that your
> motives will be misrepresented, that your patriotism will be
> impugned, that your courage will be called into question.
> But I also offer you the sure and certain knowledge that that
> we will be vindicated.

was a model of Ciceronean rhetoric, full of classical rhetorical technique, his incredulous reply was that for the whole of his professional life, 'he was a poet, but didn't know it'. Typical modesty aside, his remark illustrates that good speechwriters quickly and instinctively grasp what appeals to audiences.

To Cicero's contemporaries, the ability to understand and use these arts of oratory were the mark of a person of substance and virtue; and Cicero's descriptions of such qualities in his major rhetorical works were 'one of the formative influences on Renaissance ideals of character and education.' The sort of eloquence they described is still much valued today. But in the face-to-face, democratic city states of the classical world, before the invention of printing, the arts of oratory were not just for showing off a gentleman's education and good breeding; they were the secret to political success, and even a matter of life and death.

## 2

———————————————— ✎ ✎ ✎ ————————————————

To understand why oratory was so central to the idea of the virtuous citizen, we need to understand something about the nature of early democracy. Today it's perfectly possible (and, unfortunately, all too common) for poor orators to win elective office and even to make it all the way to the top. They may be, for instance, good backroom operators, or hardworking deputies whose turn had come, or simply lucky enough to have faced weak opponents.

But in the golden periods of classical Athens and Rome, oratory was a far more sought-after and necessary skill, whether you believed in democracy or not. Voiceless meant powerless – and vulnerable.

In 510 BC, the Athenians staged a revolution – perhaps the most influential revolution of all time – expelling its rulers, the Pisistratid tyrants. In the two-year political combat that followed, the radical aristocrat Cleisthenes outmanoeuvred his more conservative opponent Isagoras by forming an alliance with the common people – the 'demos'. In return for victory, he gave them formal control of the organs of the state. The result in 508 BC was a constitution that became described as democracy – people ('demos') power ('kratos'). In 461 BC a left-wing coup stripped the Areopagus (the conservative aristocratic council of former magistrates) of its veto over popular decision-making; the demos was now sovereign and all major political decisions were made by popular assemblies. Members of the leading families were forced to contend for power not by pleasing other members of the elite behind closed doors, but by pleasing the citizenry in public forums. Democracy had created a system of political and judicial decision-making that made persuasiveness the most powerful quality a citizen could possess. As the historian Polybius tells us, its influence later spread to Rome.

A quick survey of the workings of the constitutions of Athens and Rome at the time of Pericles and Cicero, demonstrates why oratory was so important.

**Comparison of the constitutions of Athens and Rome at the time of Pericles and Cicero**

| Athens | Rome |
|---|---|
| Legislative power | Legislative power: |
| • All adult male citizens over 20 years of age were eligible to attend meetings of the Assembly (*ekklesia*), on the hill of Pnyx, where they enjoyed freedom of speech and the right to vote by hand to pass decrees relating to foreign and domestic policy, initiate legislation by appointing a panel of legislators, elect generals and financial magistrates, and instigate political trials.<br>• All male citizens over 30 years of age were eligible to be chosen annually by lot to be one of 6000 jurors who served on panels of up to 1000 to enact new laws, decided by show of hands after a debate. | • Around 600 members of the Senate, made up of aristocratic families and former senior executive office holders, met in various buildings within the Forum to debate and pass motions on major foreign, domestic, financial and religious policy.<br>• Technically, the Senate's decisions had to be ratified by popular assemblies, which met in rowdy circumstances, often dominated by violent gangs in the pay of major power brokers, in the Comitium in the Forum or, for elections, on the Field of Mars, to enact laws, elect senior office holders, declare war and peace, and decide trials, especially political cases, involving the death penalty.<br>• Legislative measures could be vetoed by the Tribunes of the people (*tribuni plebis*), selected by the plebs to protect the common people from arbitrary actions of the upper classes. |

(*cont.*)

**Comparison of the constitutions of Athens and Rome at the time of Pericles and Cicero (*cont.*)**

| Athens | Rome |
|---|---|
| Executive power | Executive power |
| • The Council of Five Hundred (*boule*), composed of 50 men from each of the 10 tribes into which the Athenians were divided, met each day in the *bouleuterion* in the Agora to set the agenda of the Assembly and run the city's financial affairs. | • Executive power was divided between the Senate and a number of elected magistrates, most notably the consuls (of whom two were elected annually) and praetors. |
| • Executive power was also exercised by ten annually elected generals (*strategoi*), financial officers and the nine *archons* who summoned and presided over the courts and major festivals. | • During an emergency, the Senate could appoint a dictator for a period of six months or declare emergency law (*senatus consultum ultimum*) to suspend the constitution. |
| Judicial power | Judicial power |
| • Courts made up of jurors (201 and 401 for private actions and 501 or more for public actions) chosen by lot from the panel of 6000 met in the Agora to conduct public trials, including for major crimes like corruption and treason, which could carry the death penalty – accused and accusers alike were required to speak on their own behalf, with the outcome decided by a show of hands. | • Any citizen could initiate a prosecution, which would be tried before a number of separate courts, presided over by a praetor, decided by majority vote of juries drawn from the upper classes, with each side represented by one or multiple advocates. |

Cultural power

Annual festivals, games and public funerals gave members of the Athenian and Roman cultural and political elite the opportunity to impress through set-piece oratory. After the fall of the democracy and the Republic, such events were the only opportunities for meaningful public speech, and their subject matter was closely monitored.

Pericles – the first great political orator. Photo: © kmiragaya/Shutter-
stock.com.

A public figure in Athens or Rome would have to be adept
at speaking in a variety of settings: in front of hundreds of fellow
citizens in meetings of the Council of Five Hundred or Senate to
control the administration of the state; in front of many thousands
at the assemblies on the Pnyx, at the comitia, or on the Field of
Mars and in defence of his very life in front of juries of between 30
and 10 000.

Think of the contrast with today. The overwhelming majority
of our political class – the backroom advisers who often squeeze
their way onto party nomination lists – not only have little opportunity to speak in public, but they are also usually forbidden from
doing so. During election campaigns all but the party leadership
are sometimes gagged to prevent them speaking at all. Elected
representatives engage directly with voters so infrequently that
when they do it is often regarded as a stunt or a public relations

gimmick – think of the confected town hall meetings the campaign teams like so much. If we are unlucky enough to end up in court, a highly paid barrister does the talking for us, constrained by court procedures designed to stamp out appeals based on stretched logic and obvious emotion.

Not so in the ancient world. Straightforward, calm, rational forums for debate – that was the constitutional intent anyway. The reality was much rougher.

We've already seen Cicero in chapter 1 complaining about having to address a Senate surrounded by Antony's soldiers. It was an extreme example, but to be expected in the tough world of public speaking. Audiences, made up in large part of the uneducated, were easily bored, rude and even abusive. One of the greatest Greek orators, Demosthenes, bitterly recounted how his chief enemies once positioned themselves on either side of the speaking platform to mock him, to the great amusement of the crowd. Even Pericles – perhaps the greatest Athenian politician of them all – had to regularly endure the taunts of persistent hecklers, who would sometimes continue the onslaught throughout his journey home. Character assassination often took the place of factual argument, and it wasn't unusual for orators to be accused, as Demosthenes was, of betrayal of his friends, being the passive partner in a homosexual encounter, behaving as a coward in battle, and failing to respect the gods.

In fact, politics was more corrupt and violent than today, and captured by a political class of wealthy or politically able men, who could, like Pericles and Caesar, have popular sympathies, or like Alcibiades and Cicero, elite ones. It's not difficult to see how for such men – and for any brave citizen willing to stand up and be counted – the consequences of failure to be persuasive could be humiliating and catastrophic. And not just for them. In one of the most famous debates of classical times, a fierce tussle in the Athenian Assembly in 427 BC between the orators Cleon and Diodotus, only just managed to rescind a motion calling for the execution of the entire adult male population of the rebel city state of Mytilene and the enslavement of its women and children. Speaking up was dangerous. This was especially so when one considers that prosecutions were often politically motivated; that juries and assemblies could be bribed, stacked with intimidating thugs and professional demonstrators, and composed of social classes hostile to either side; and that failure could bring severe fines, exile or even a ghastly death through garrotting, being thrown off a cliff, or being placed in a sack and drowned in the Tiber.

On occasions though, oratory could bring much acclaim and wealth. Having the honour of delivering a major public address – as Pericles famously did in his Funeral Oration of 430 BC – could mark a man with greatness. The very best professional public speakers often enjoyed similar wealth and fame as do entertainment personalities today.

Clearly, oratory was a skill a citizen neglected at his peril.

# 3

❧ ❧ ❧

Someone who paid the price for scorning oratory was the Greek philosopher Socrates.

In one of the most famous political trials of all time, Socrates was accused in 399 BC of 'not acknowledging the gods the city acknowledges' and of 'corrupting the young'. It is likely that the charges had their roots in the philosopher's mistrust of the city's democracy and his close associations with aristocratic counter-revolutionaries whose death squads had terrorised the city and who had aligned themselves traitorously with Athens' enemy, Sparta. It's a story often told, but its importance for our purposes is Socrates' stubborn refusal to defend himself or mitigate the severity of his sentence by appealing to the sympathies of the jury. To Socrates, oratory's use of emotion to sway juries was childish and demeaning to grown men. The only correct action for a rational person to take was to appeal to a jury's reason and principles, which he proceeded to do, daring the jury not only to convict him but also to impose the penalty of death through the drinking of hemlock.

[Y]ou shall hear from me nothing but the truth. Not . . . speeches finely tricked out with words and phrases . . . nor carefully arranged, but you will hear things said at random with the words that happen to occur to me. For I trust that what I say is just; and let none of you expect anything else. For surely it would not be fitting for one of my age to come before you like a youngster making up speeches . . . I make this request of you . . . that you disregard the manner of my speech . . . and observe and pay attention merely to this, whether what I say is just or not . . .

[Jurymen] either acquit me, or not, knowing that I shall not change my conduct even if I am to die many times over.

[I]f you put me to death, you will not easily find another, who, to use a rather absurd figure, attaches himself to the city as a gadfly to a horse, which, though large and well bred, is sluggish . . . and needs to be aroused by stinging. I think the gods fastened me upon the city in some such capacity, and I go about arousing, and urging and reproaching each one of you, constantly alighting upon you everywhere the whole day long. Such another is not likely to come to you . . . [I]f you take my advice, you will spare me. But you, perhaps, might be angry, like people awakened from a nap, and might slap me, as Anytus advises, and easily kill me . . .

Perhaps some one among you may be offended when he remembers his own conduct, if he, even in a case of less importance than this, begged and besought the judges with many tears, and brought forward his children to arouse compassion . . . I will do none of these things, though I am, apparently, in the very greatest danger. Perhaps some one with these thoughts in mind may be harshly disposed toward me and may cast his vote in anger. Now if any one of you is so disposed . . . I think I should be speaking fairly if I said to him, 'My friend, I too have relatives . . . but nevertheless I shall not bring any of them here and beg you to acquit me.' And why shall I not do so? Not because I am stubborn . . . or lack respect for you . . . [Y]ou should make it clear that you will be much more ready to condemn a man who puts before you such pitiable scenes and makes the city ridiculous than one who keeps quiet.

Later, having been found guilty, Socrates responds to the question of what sentence he thinks should be imposed.

What, then, does such a man as I deserve? . . . I propose maintenance in the prytaneum [i.e. at the public's expense].

After the jury subsequently votes for the death sentence, Socrates concludes:

You would have liked to hear me wailing and lamenting and doing and saying many things which are . . . unworthy of me . . . [But] I much prefer to die after such a defence than to live after a defence of the other sort.

Socrates' defence (if it could be called that) was admirable for its courage, but it was also doomed. For the budding politician, his speech is a textbook study in how *not* to win friends and influence people. It may have worked perhaps in the rarefied atmosphere of the Academy, as it might today in university seminar rooms, where those who participate in the daily grind of democratic politics are often viewed with barely polite condescension.

Outside the Academy, though, it was doomed to failure. In essence his plea came down to this: jurymen, if you were wise and brave you would acquit me, but as you are intellectually lazy and cowardly, and because I refuse to lower myself to appeal to your irrational emotions, you will no doubt convict; and if you do, you had better impose capital punishment, because should I live, I will continue to flout your laws and insult you.

Anyone who has worked in politics for any length of time would have come across people like Socrates, who manage to combine a bleak view of their fellow man with rather unworldly idealism. The history books warm to them, but in a practical way they tend to achieve little except martyrdom, especially when up against a ruthless opponent.

# 4

Cicero, however, knew better.

It's often said that every great term of office has a good crisis. Churchill had 1940. All Bill Clinton had was rising prosperity. Cicero was luckier. Upon being elected as consul for 63 BC (admittedly from a weak field, and aided by a timely economic crisis), Cicero was faced with a major conspiracy against the Roman state led by a desperate, foolish and careless aristocrat, Lucius Sergius Catilina, whom he had just defeated in the consular elections. Taken at face value, the evidence suggests that Cicero had an open and shut case against Catilina, backed up by the testimony of informants and intercepted correspondence detailing a provincial uprising and march on Rome to massacre opponents and install a revolutionary government that would cancel debts and redistribute property. Others familiar with recent politics and emergency anti-terrorist legislation suggest a more sinister interpretation of Cicero's actions – the manufacturing of exaggerated threats to set a trap for naïve opponents.

> Certainly the failure of Cicero's aristocratic allies to address the poverty and corruption in Rome at the time would have given Catiline's attempt some degree of moral legitimacy and popular support and enable some to portray him not as a monster but a doomed idealist.

Either way, Cicero was convinced that his chance at fame, if not his life and the safety of the city, were at stake. He could be a subtle and idealistic philosopher, and at times weak and a 'trimmer', but when it counted, he was prepared to strike and use brutal argumentation to destroy his opponents.

In four preserved speeches from the time – some of which were obviously improved before publication a few years later – Cicero, speaking from the Senate chair and the Rostra in the Forum, drove Catilina from Rome and finally, with the help of a celebrated speech from the stoic Marcus Porcius Cato, convinced the Senate to execute the leading conspirators. Of these, the most remembered is the first, with its famous lines:

> *Quo usque tandem abutere, Catilina, patientia nostra?*
> How long, Catilina, do you propose to try our patience?
> *O tempora, o mores!*
> What scandalous times we live in!

A sentence so pervasive in its influence that it (perhaps unwittingly) finds its way into rock music, as in this lyric from Midnight Oil's song 'The Power and the Passion': 'Oh, the power and the passion. Oh, the temper of the times!' Perhaps not coincidentally, its singer-songwriter went on to become a politician.

The writer Robert Harris, who turned Cicero's life into a series of popular and convincing novels, has dramatised the events of the Catiline conspiracy. His handling of the first speech (which is as true as fiction needs to be to the original text, and provides some realistic insight into the making of a truly dramatic speech, recounted supposedly through the eyes of Cicero's secretary Tiro) gives us a good feel for the drama of the moment, in which Catiline had unwisely attended the meeting of the Senate to face down his accusers, only to find his co-senators forsake him by moving and leaving him sitting on his own.

> Cicero was fiddling with a roll of papyrus. He turned to find
> out what was happening and I saw his face transfix with
> astonishment. I spun around in alarm myself – only to see
> Catilina calmly taking his place on one of the benches.
> Almost everyone else was still on their feet, watching him.
> Catilina sat, whereupon all the men nearest to him started
> edging away, as if he had leprosy. I never saw such a
> demonstration in my life. Even Caesar wouldn't go near

him. Catilina took no notice, but folded his arms and thrust out his chin. The silence lengthened, until eventually I heard Cicero's voice, very calm, behind me.

'How much longer, Catilina, will you try our patience?'

All my life people have asked me about Cicero's speech that day. 'Did he write it out beforehand?' they want to know. 'Surely he must at least have planned what he wanted to say?' The answer to both questions is 'no'. It was entirely spontaneous. Fragments of things he had long wanted to say, lines he had practised in his head, thoughts that had come to him. In the sleepless nights of the past few months – all of it wove together while he was on his feet.

'How much longer must we put up with your madness?'

He descended from his dais and started to advance very slowly along the aisle to where Catilina was sitting. As he walked, he extended both his arms and briefly gestured to the senators to take their places, which they did, and somehow that schoolmasterly gesture, and their instant compliance, established his authority. He was speaking for the republic.

'Is there no end to your arrogance? Don't you understand that we know what you're up to? Don't you appreciate that your conspiracy is uncovered? Don't you think there's a man among us who doesn't know what you did last night – where you were, who came to your meeting, and what you agreed?' He stood at last in front of Catilina, his arms akimbo, looked him up and down, and shook his head. 'Oh what times are these,' he said in a voice of utter disgust, 'and oh, what morals! The senate knows everything, the consul knows everything, and yet – *this man is still alive*!'

He wheeled around. 'Alive? Not just alive, gentlemen,' he cried, moving on down the aisle from Catilina and addressing the packed benches from the centre of the temple, 'he attends the Senate! He takes part in our debates. He listens to us. He watches us – and all the time he's deciding who he going to kill! Is this how we serve the Republic – simply by sitting here, hoping it's going to be us? How very brave we are! It's been twenty days since we voted ourselves the authority to act. We have the sword – but we keep it sheathed! You ought to have been executed immediately, Catilina. Yet still you live. And as long as you live, you don't give up plotting – you increase it!'

I suppose by now even Catilina must have realised the size of his mistake in coming into the temple. In terms of physical strength and sheer effrontery he was much more powerful than Cicero. But the senate was not the arena for brute force. The weapons here were words, and no one ever knew how to deploy words as well as Cicero. For twenty years, whenever the courts were in session, scarcely a day had gone by that hadn't seen Cicero practising his craft. In a sense, his whole life had been a preparation for this moment.

Oratory saved Cicero's life and the Republic – this time.

# 5

With so much at stake, most souls (with the exception of Socrates, obviously) looking down from the Pnyx or the Rostra to the rowdy audience below would have had many things going through their minds other than the simple righteousness or logicality of their cause:

- How do I grab the audience's attention and hold it?
- How can I be convincing without sounding too polished, phony or superior?
- How do I get my largely illiterate audience to care about a well-educated elite like me and what I have to say?
- How do I get my main point over most effectively?

- What arguments are most likely to work in this particular situation?
- How do I make my most telling points stick?
- What will make them take what I say at face value, especially as my facts are, to say the least, debateable?

What were the answers? Were there short cuts to success and potential greatness?

Given to philosophising, the Greeks and Romans began noticing that, circumstances being similar, some speaking methods tended to achieve more success than others. They quickly concluded that, given men's minds seemed to respond to verbal stimuli in predictable ways, there must be an art to success in public speaking. And, being great systematisers, they began noticing patterns. Speeches could be grouped into similar types. They all tended to have the same basic components. Their speakers had the same limited number of tasks. And each audience and occasion demanded an appropriate style of drafting and delivery. A science, or perhaps more accurately, an art (or even trade) of oratory was created.

Many handbooks were written. While the major classical authorities varied in their emphasis and comprehensiveness, we can separate their major understandings about classical rhetoric into four major areas: the types of speeches (the 'classification'), the parts of each speech (the 'divisions'), the tasks of the speaker (the 'canons'), and the appropriate style to be adopted.

---

**The four major areas of classical rhetoric**

---

**The types of speeches**

There are three basic types or classifications of speeches:

- *forensic* – a legal speech in a law court
- *deliberative* – a political speech in an executive council, legislature or public assembly

**The parts of speech**

There are five basic parts or divisions of speech:

- the *prologue* – the opening remarks that grab the audience's attention and sympathies
- the *narrative* – the speaker's major contention or case
- the *proofs* – the arguments used to support the speaker's contention or case

- *display* – a speech in praise of others, such as a eulogy, or a formal occasion for showing off the speaker's eloquence.
- *refutation* – refuting the arguments of the opposing case
- *conclusion* – summing up or ending by cinching the case or ramming the major points home.

## The orator's tasks

The orator has five main tasks (or canons of speech):

- *invention* – the discovery of useful arguments ('what to say')
- *disposition* – the arrangement of the arguments for maximum effect ('how to set it out')
- *elocution* – employing the right rhetorical style to give the delivery extra force ('how to say it')
- *memory* – memorisation (crucial in the age before the word processor and the autocue) ('how to remember it without reading')
- *pronunciation* – delivery ('how to deliver it on the night').

## The style to be adopted

Each speech has a delivery most appropriate to the audience and occasion:

- *the plain style* – a direct and concise way of speaking, stripped of all obvious rhythm, ornament and emotion; designed to be clear rather than impressive; sometimes intentionally delivered to sound untrained
- *the middle style* – emphasises argument and content; can be stylish and contain emotion, but in a restrained way; charming rather than vigorous
- *the grand style* – the most forceful style of speaking, in which the power of the argument is matched by the majesty of the diction; employs every relevant oratorical device to arouse the audience and sway its emotions; can be rough and severe, smooth and charming or high toned and principled, depending on the needs of the speaker.

While technology and fashion have influenced oratory since these insights were first developed, they remain invaluable.

Given the importance of oratory, it is hardly surprising that some of the finest minds of first Greek and then Roman civilisation set out to tell ambitious men its secrets. An oratory industry quickly grew around this knowledge. And like all such advice industries it had its share of hype and celebrity gurus able to attract huge fees – for Aristotle, think of Peter Drucker; for Gorgias, Richard Florida.

As we have seen, the preconditions for the flourishing of Athenian oratory had been created by a democratic revolution, but they were aided by the threat to democracy in another city. In 427 BC the orators Gorgias and Teisias from the Sicilian city of Leontini, who were followers of a certain Corax (reputedly the founder of the systematic study of oratory), led a delegation to Athens to plead for their city's support against its enemy Syracuse. Gorgias' speech to the Assembly on the Pnyx, followed by a number of display speeches to round off his tour, caused a sensation among the politically literate population through their use of a new type of rhythmic prose. Everyone wanted to copy it – or found it impossible not to. As any political speechwriter will tell you, the subject matter, arguments, style and rhythms of every new political sensation quickly work their way into their bosses' speeches. New styles become ubiquitous. Sometimes this happens by choice. In the way women not long ago went to the hair salon to ask for 'a Jennifer Aniston', in the 1960s every politician wanted 'a John F. Kennedy', in the 1990s 'a Tony Blair', and in the 2000s 'a Barack Obama'. But at other times it is involuntary. Think of the way rock'n'roll changed sharply following the arrival of the Beatles' new sound: by getting inside the heads of singers, song writers and listeners, it changed music forever. A similar thing happened to oratory in the Greek world.

And as with us, the Greeks were willing to pay for the advantages that the possession of a new type of knowledge gave them. Fees for a full course from the leading instructors in oratory could cost 100 minae, which one historian has estimated in 2003 as the equivalent of as much as £160 000 (US$260 000, €185 000, or A$290 000) – which makes a full-fee degree from an Ivy League university seem almost a bargain by comparison. Gorgias came back on repeat tours to Athens to be the main draw card at the biggest festivals, such as the Pan Hellenic Games and the Olympics, where public oratory was part of the mixture of religion, education and entertainment.

From then on, public speaking was never the same. Instead of speaking off the cuff, people began speaking in the most elaborate ways, the sense of which can be gained from this extract from one of Gorgias' surviving orations, The encomium of Helen – which considered the reasons why Helen went to Troy to start the Trojan War.

> [6] For either it was     by the will of Fate
>            and     the wishes of the Gods
>            and     the votes of Necessity
> that she did what she did,
>            or     by force reduced
>            or     by words seduced
>          <or     by love possessed.>
> Now if through the first,
>      it is right for the responsible to be held responsible;
>      for God's predetermination cannot be hindered
>          by human premeditation.
> For it is the nature of things,
>      not for the stronger to be hindered by the weaker,
>      but for the weaker to be ruled and drawn by the stronger,
>      and for the stronger to lead     and the weaker to follow.
> God is a stronger force than man
>      in might and in wit     and in other ways.
> If then on Fate and on God one must place blame
> Helen from disgrace must be set free

One can see how such manner of public speaking would soon be open to ridicule, especially after being taken to its logical extremes by less talented disciples, and in fact both Aristotle and Cicero held it up as an example of what *not* to do. But, in less effete form, a number of Gorgias' public speaking techniques survived the changing fashions down to today.

Gorgias, though, was merely the most famous of other travelling philosophers and teachers of oratory who converged on Athens. Others included Protagoras from Abdera, Prodicus from Ceos and Hippias from Elis. The hunger for instruction and the fantastic amounts of money to be made, unsurprisingly, spurred the foundation of competing schools and celebrity instructors, complete with their own fashionable theories and handbooks, each with their own unique selling point, looking to establish a niche in a marketplace in which even the slightest edge in swaying an audience could be decisive. Much like our leading consulting houses today – for the Sophists, think of McKinsey Consulting; for the Academy, Boston Consulting.

Busy men of action being what they are, one day they began paying others to write speeches for them. The professional speech-writer, the *logographoi*, had been created – the first of whom was probably the *metic* (non-citizen) Lysias, forced to sell his eloquence in the political marketplace after losing his fortune during Athens' political calamities at the end of the 5th century BC.

Things of course went too far, and the resulting excess also produced satire and academic criticism. The targets were a disparate group of freelance intellectuals known collectively as Sophists. The term originally meant something similar to our word 'expert', but soon acquired the connotation it has had ever since: a nitpicker, a shallow pseudo-intellectual, a mere technical expert who is adept at the skill of argument and will plead any case for the right money. To the playwright Aristophanes, Sophists were dangerous because they could make 'the weaker argument the stronger' and, by arming the young and the uneducated with effective debating tactics, undermine tradition and social stability. And to Plato, who established the Academy in part to oppose the Sophists, they taught mere technical, self-interested knowledge instead of the true vocation of the philosopher, the disinterested search for the truth. In doing so, Plato anticipated the criticisms members of today's academy commonly make against their rivals in political think tanks and management consultancy firms. In Plato's ideal world, ruled by philosopher statesmen, there would be no need for oratory because leaders would rule through the application of reason alone. It seems what the Sophists lacked in terms of academic credibility they more than made up for in insights about the corrupting nature of unlimited power. They may well have been shallow, cynical and even venal, and the results of their teachings may have been messy, irrational and sometimes dangerous in the wrong hands, but by teaching people how to speak in public the Sophists provided a valuable service to the cause of democracy, which, contrary to Plato, has proved the only practical antidote ever devised against tyranny – with the exception, in desperate times, of the knife and the gun.

# 6

❧ ❧ ❧

While Plato opposed the teaching of oratory altogether, one of his students, Aristotle, had a slightly different view. Aristotle too was an anti-democrat, believing democracy wrongly appealed to people's passions rather than their reason, potentially giving power to the mob, but he thought it important to understand how persuasion worked and how it could be turned to the aid of reason and justice. Until now sophistic writers had circulated numerous 'how to' manuals on oratory, none of which survive in full. Turning his philosophical genius to the subject, Aristotle produced the earliest truly significant theory and system of oratory to survive until today, *The art of rhetoric*. To modern readers Aristotle's book is a far from easy going, but can be thought of as answering two concerns central to oratory:

1 *why* be persuasive
2 *how* to be persuasive.

The first, which can be taken as a refutation of the extreme anti-rhetoric stance of Plato, is answered by pointing out that oratory is in fact a different category altogether to pure philosophy. It is perhaps best explained by this simple grid, which contrasts the tool of philosophy (logic) with that of oratory (rhetoric) when it comes to proving or winning an argument.

**Winning or losing arguments through the use of philosophy and oratory**

| Philosophy | Oratory |
|---|---|
| academic | practical |
| its arguments use logical reasoning | its arguments apply logic to real life |
| its conclusions are irrefutable and apply in every case | its conclusions are debateable and apply to particular cases |
| there is no audience | the audience decides |

In other words, persuasion through oratory is a practical form of philosophising, and, unlike philosophy, one concerned with the reactions of its audience. Hence Aristotle's next argument that an orator must understand the state of mind of the audience and how to appeal to it through the mastery of particular styles, techniques and competency in delivery. Aristotle's major contribution to the understanding of oratory was his acknowledgement that (sadly, in his opinion and that of his colleagues at the Academy) in the court of public opinion, logic does not provide the only form of proof of a speaker's case. There are three forms of proof:

1  logic (*logos*) – the logical coherency of the speaker's case, backed by evidence
2  emotion (*pathos*) – the successful appeal to the audience's emotions
3  character (*ethos*) – the creation of trust in what the speaker says.

Cicero agreed. The best speechwriters and orators, he insisted, are not necessarily those who know the most about their subject, or who know the rules of speaking, or who are the most passionate. The best orators are those who understand the needs of their audience and employ the right combination of logic, character and emotion to convince, charm and sway it. Each speaking occasion has its own requirements and success needs sound judgement on the part of the speaker to produce a speech apt for the occasion. As

Cicero tells us, the ideal orator is one who 'can discuss common-place matters simply, lofty subjects impressively, and topics ranging between in a tempered style'.

While Aristotle's work on oratory was groundbreaking, it was far from comprehensive or coherent. Over the following four centuries his theories about oratory were developed into the categories still largely used to understand it today. As we have seen, Cicero was a major contributor to this enterprise, although one concerned more with the development of an artistic style and with the linking of oratory to the cause of liberty than with the creation of a system or curriculum. But in the same way that the romantic revolutionary Karl Marx's works were often simplified and clarified for the general reader by his friend and disciple Friedrich Engels, Aristotle's insights and Cicero's romantic political defence of oratory were systematised for following generations by Cicero's admirer Marcus Fabius Quintilian.

# 7

The son of an orator, Quintilian was born in Spain in 35 AD, subsequently moving to Rome during the reign of the Emperor Nero to be educated by leading rhetoricians. His own school of rhetoric was extremely successful, counting among its students the Younger Pliny and the historian Tacitus (whose dark histories of the period provided the raw material for the Robert Graves *I Claudius* novels and subsequent television series, which illustrate how completely the republican world of Cicero's time had disappeared).

His school also brought him unusual wealth for a teacher, aided most likely by his closeness to successive emperors and by the fact that he was the first teacher of rhetoric to be paid a salary by the state. The irony of his position couldn't have been lost on Quintilian: there he was, inheritor of Cicero's mission to pursue liberty through heroic oratory, advising a corrupt state that made meaningful oratory all but impossible. It's a trap all professional speechwriters recognise: the blacker the cause, the higher the fee.

Given the moral compromises this must have required, Quintilian did the only practical and honourable thing: he retired while still at the height of his powers to write a book setting out the rules of oratory perhaps for future generations to one day uncover in the cause of freedom.

The book, *Institutio oratoria* ('Training in oratory') was an encyclopaedic reference, which drew on the works of Cicero and the Greek masters, to set out almost every conceivable aspect of how to educate and train the perfect orator, from the youngest child to the mature man: how to train his voice, how he should dress, what gestures he should employ at the Rostra, and, inevitably for a disciple of Cicero, what sort of man he should be – 'a man of the highest character and ideals, the consummation of all that is best in morals, training and stylistic discernment'. Importantly, Quintilian discussed at length the technical aspects of speech contained in the works of the Greek and Roman masters to provide a definitive summation of how classical oratory should be understood.

Lost to all but monks and assorted scholars for centuries, we should think of *Institutio oratoria* as a buried time capsule containing a guide to how to be a complete citizen in a world of liberty. When it was found in a monastery in St Gallen by the humanist scholar Poggio Bracciolini in 1416, part of the same enthusiasm that led to successful hunts for the lost works of Cicero, 'it became a guiding text of a new cultural revolution that redefined not just what literature meant, but what it meant to be an educated person in a free society'. And as we have seen, the contents of Quintilian's, Cicero's and their interpreters' books reshaped the education systems of the early modern world, leaving their rhetorical legacies to us via the works of Shakespeare.

In the chapters that follow, we are going to apply the insights developed by the classical thinkers and systematised by Quintilian to examine a selection of the greatest and most familiar speeches of history to demonstrate how the speakers and speechwriters go about this task of winning a case, winning power or winning acclaim.

We are going to see how the great speeches are memorable for a reason: consciously or unconsciously, through training or instinct, their speechwriters and speakers follow the basic techniques set out by the classical authorities more than 2000 years ago. And this includes the best speakers of our own age – Barack Obama and Sarah Palin.

# Chapter 3
# **Forum**

## 1

❧ ❧ ❧

Where does a speechwriter start when a brief lands on his or her desk? As Cicero tells us, the first task is to find out who will be in the forum. Know your audience.

## 2

❧ ❧ ❧

Stepping onto the Moon on 21 July 1969, astronaut Neil Armstrong delivered one of the most remembered one-line speeches of all time. Even though he fluffed its delivery (leaving out a crucial indefinite article), it remains a memorable case of antithesis.

That's one small step for [a] man; one giant leap for mankind.

Armstrong's words survive for one reason: the world, literally, was watching. Seen live by some 450 million television viewers, the astronaut had the undivided attention of what was, until that time, probably the biggest audience in human history. He held the ultimate forum – humanity at the moment of its most stunning technological achievement. (And, as we shall see elsewhere in the book, the Apollo program provided the moments for some of the twentieth century's most inspiring rhetoric.)

The moon landing speech illustrates the supreme importance for the orator of seizing the moment. Armstrong could justifiably have said nothing. In the frenzy following the rocket launch and preparation for the moonwalk, the question of what to say could easily have been overlooked. The technocrats at NASA may easily have regarded words as a distracting indulgence better left for the post-return-to-Earth press conference. This belief – that when all's said and done words don't really matter – is common but it is also a mistake. Even in politics, complex policy ideas launched without enough care given to their description and defence have a habit of not leaving the ground. Thankfully, Armstrong knew this. Somewhere between Earth and the Moon, he found the time to clear his mind and think of what to say. And it was brilliant.

## 3

Not all speeches can coincide with world historical events. The most important speeches invariably do, and truly great speeches, including many of those discussed in this book, match those events with such force and style that they help change history. But to be judged a success, every speech needs an essential element: a forum. I'm not talking just about the physical meeting places (named after the Roman Forum) where orators address their audiences, or even the composition of the audience itself, but something less concrete, concerned with the quality of the connection between the speaker and the crowd – a quality that makes the audience members bend their heads towards the speaker and keep them there. It has two essential elements:

1   The first is a sense of anticipation generated by the importance of the occasion or the reputation of the speaker.

2  But such moments can be fluffed, so the second element is an appropriate combination of seriousness, intensity, argument, emotion and style (a combination known as *decorum*) apt for the particular time, place and circumstances (or *kairos*) of the speech.

The audience must have a reason for tuning in and a reason for not tuning out. In short, a good speech must have a forum and hold it. In the same way philosophers have asked whether a tree really falls in a forest when nobody hears it fall, it can be asked whether a speech is really made when there's nobody really listening. No forum, no speech.

It's sometimes difficult to measure the extent to which a politician has the forum. But it is obvious when they don't. Again, Cicero knew:

> An expert who understands the principles of oratory does
> not need to sit down and listen attentively to what is being
> said. Instead, by a single passing glance at the audience, he
> can usually tell how good the speaker is. Let us imagine he
> sees one of the jurymen yawning, talking to one of his
> colleagues, perhaps even chatting to a group of them,
> sending out to discover what time it is, asking the presiding
> officer to declare an adjournment. When the expert notes all
> this, he realizes that this is a lawsuit in which the speaker is
> not capable of playing on the hearts of the court, as the
> hand of a musician plays on his strings. But if, on the
> contrary, he notices that the jurymen are concentrating
> attentively, and look as though they are trying to learn what
> the case is about, or are visibly displaying their assent by
> their facial expressions, or hanging upon the words of the
> speaker like birds entranced by the siren songs of a
> catcher . . . he will already be able to understand perfectly
> well that an authentic orator is in action in that court.

Every experienced speechwriter, political adviser and political reporter knows, usually to their pain, when a forum is missing.

Take a typical party conference. Even the dullest and most stage-managed has a debate that brings tensions to a head. It may be on a seemingly humdrum issue of interest to only the most committed wonk – trade policy perhaps – but it's really about power: who can command the floor; whether the leadership can stare down a challenge to its authority. The delegates flood in and take their seats, listening intently to every word, clapping and cheering as the major thrusts are made. Then it's over. The chair declares the vote, and calls the mover of the next item of business. One of the party's solid performers then gets to his feet to approach the rostrum, armed with a well-crafted and highly considered speech . . . only to find that the delegates are already on their way to the lobby to get a coffee and discuss the outcome of the crucial debate. Audiences are not good at faking attention. The speaker just isn't that famous; the debate not consequential enough; it won't make the evening news. He speaks to an empty hall. There is no forum.

Sometimes the sudden disappearance of a forum can spell the end for a faltering politician. Like the sand rushing through an hourglass, an audience making for the exits usually signals that a leader's time is up. Like all speechwriters, I've experienced this first-hand.

No decision is more consequential for a democracy, and no moment so crucial for a politician than declaring war. As we saw in chapter 2, the commitment of troops to Vietnam in 1965 provided the occasion for Australian Labor leader Arthur Calwell, aided by speechwriter Graham Freudenberg, to make one of the finest speeches in Australian political history. Despite always being an improbable prime minister, Calwell at least went down in the history books as a passionate opponent of what turned out to be a disastrous war. On 22 January 2003, the Australian Government announced it would send troops to the Middle East as part of the build up for the second Iraq war. The then Labor leader, Simon Crean, was presented with his chance. And he started well. As his speechwriter, I was involved in the discussions about his response. He decided to use the occasion of the embarkation of the departing troops the following day to state his position in a dramatic fashion, by standing on the gun deck of the departing troopship and telling the troops firmly that while he wished them God's speed for a safe return, he opposed their deployment:

> I don't want to mince my words because I don't believe that you should be going. I don't think that there should be a deployment of troops to Iraq ahead of the United Nations determining it. But that's a political decision . . . You don't have a choice and my argument is with the government, not with you.

The sentiment was based on Crean's own experiences of having seen friends who had been conscripted to fight in Vietnam come back damaged. It was a powerful statement that displayed considerable political courage, which, for a while, had the poorly polling Crean on the side of the majority. Crean was no great orator, but he proved that even limited speakers can capture attention and gain widespread respect by displaying strong character, standing on deeply held principle and seizing the moment when people are listening. But while the speech may have made some take a second and more favourable look at Crean, his leadership was in terminal decline, and in such circumstances it doesn't take much to make an audience switch off. Two weeks later he faltered in the parliamentary debate on the troop deployment, departing from a crisp and strongly worded set of speaking notes to engage in an elaborate and repetitive discussion of the authority of the United Nations (making the mistake, as we will discuss in chapter 7, of choosing a *forensic* speech when he should have made a *deliberative* one). Watching from the advisers' box on the floor of the House of Representatives, I can recall first the backbench, then Crean's own frontbench colleagues start to fidget, talk and, one by one, absent themselves from the chamber. It was the beginning of the end for his leadership. A further two weeks on, Crean unwisely told a peace rally that while he opposed the war, he would support it if the United Nations sanctioned it. While appropriate to an audience of soldiers and sailors, the Labor leader's message was wrong for an audience dominated by a band of noisy and radical anti-war activists. The crowd booed. Unable to command even those who mostly agreed with him, Crean had lost his forum, and was effectively finished. As often happens in such situations the real political action now took place not in public debates but in the backrooms as the plotters began their work.

# 4

History is littered with similar failures to take the forum by making the most of a major historical occasion. One thinks of George W. Bush's declaration of 'mission accomplished' on the deck of the aircraft carrier, USS *Abraham Lincoln*, on 1 May 2003. Or perhaps of Mikhail Gorbachev's aimless public appearances upon his release from house arrest after the collapse of the August 1991 coup – a failure that saw him supplanted by Boris Yeltsin, who, in the days previously, had defiantly and dramatically addressed Russia from the top of an armoured vehicle to demand the release of Gorbachev and a general strike. Perhaps not coincidentally, Lenin had done exactly the same thing upon his return to Petrograd on 3 April 1917 following the success of the February revolution. Yeltsin may have later been exposed as a fool, but he knew how to seize one of the most consequential moments in the twentieth century to bring down a tottering, corrupt empire.

Every day, in fact, political orators misjudge their forum and lose it – presenting, say, a press club full of cynical political reporters hungry for news and drama, with a shopping list of worthy policies or achievements. This is why the experienced speechwriter starts by assessing the audience. Armed with the right sort of experience and knowledge, he or she will intuitively know how to appeal to those listening, make the moment work and, if they're good, hit it out of the park. Like a batter saving his best innings for the World Series or the Cricket World Cup Final, the great orators save their best speeches for the most important occasions.

Boris Yeltsin, imitating Lenin, brings down a corrupt empire. Photo: © AFP/Getty Images.

How, though, do we interpret the moment?

It helps to know your history and literature. To the politically active these disciplines are a source of knowledge, perspective, examples, and common forms of argument – what Aristotle called *topoi* – that enable a speechwriter to interpret unfolding events and make informed judgements about what to say and do. In this way they give speechwriters and speechmakers the capacity to grasp the true significance of a political moment so they can respond with a speech both apt and memorable. One of Cicero's most famous quotes was made while proving his point that the best orators are those who have studied history.

To be ignorant of what occurred before you were born is to remain always a child.

The politicians who won the Battle of Britain are proof of this. They were the beneficiaries of an education system that took history and literature seriously. Like so much associated with great speeches, the highly consequential debates and prime ministerial addresses of the spring and summer of 1940 have their origins in the age of Shakespeare.

On Wednesday 7 May 1940 the House of Commons began debating the innocuous sounding motion 'That this house do now adjourn'. It was a very indirect, very British, way of conducting a parliamentary inquest into the humiliating military defeat in Norway, and quickly turned into a test of the Chamberlain government's parliamentary numbers, which the historian and former politician Roy Jenkins has described as being

> by a clear head both the most dramatic and most
> far-reaching in its consequences of any parliamentary debate
> of the twentieth century. It was also one in which nearly
> every MP who occupied or sought first rank took part . . .

One of those in the first rank who made a telling contribution was Admiral of the Fleet Sir Roger Keyes, a supporter of the then First Sea Lord Winston Churchill's bolder and more adventurous approach to strategy, who used the occasion to advocate subtly and indirectly for a change of government to be led by Churchill. Dressed for the occasion in full admiral's uniform and medals to reinforce that he was speaking for the navy, Keyes ended his speech, as Jenkins records, 'by playing on the most obvious but nonetheless evocative chord in naval history: "One hundred and forty years ago Nelson said, 'I am of the opinion that the boldest measures are the safest', and that still holds good today."' Invoking Nelson – the hero of Trafalgar, who saved Britain from invasion by Napoleon – signalled the significance of the historical moment of the debate.

But an even more historically loaded and forceful rhetorical blow was landed in the same debate by a renegade Tory Leo Amery. To understand its point and impact we need to digress for a moment and go back to the 1640s and 1650s. During those two decades, England experienced a revolution, involving two major civil wars, the execution of the king, the abolition of the House of Lords, the establishment of a republic and the eventual restoration of the monarchy. The driving force of the revolution was the parliamentary army commanded by Oliver Cromwell. Cromwell believed in a hierarchy of talent and godliness, and, believing that fighting spirit not social rank was the only criterion for the selection of his armoured cavalry, famously remarked that: 'I had rather have a plain russet-coated captain that knows what he fights for, and loves what he knows, than that which you call a gentleman and is nothing else.'

By 1653 these godly and committed Ironsides had grown impatient of the Long Parliament, which was unable to make a decision about its dissolution and replacement with a new form of republican government that would protect the revolution from its royalist enemies. On 20 April, now totally fed up with the Long Parliament's indecision, Cromwell, assisted by a squad of musketeers, entered the chamber of the House of Commons and dissolved it with these well-known words: 'It is not fit that you should sit here any longer. You have sat here too long for any good you have been doing lately. Depart, I say, and let us have done with you. In the name of God, go.' By the end of the year, Cromwell was the Lord Protector, the first ever republican head of state in the British Isles.

Like Nelson's most famous lines, Cromwell's were known by every English public schoolboy – including Leo Amery and the MPs listening to the debate on 7 and 8 May 1940. Here is Amery's diary entry about his most famous and decisive parliamentary speech:

I looked up my favourite old quotation of Cromwell's about his selection of Ironsides and then remembered his other quotation when he dismissed the Long Parliament. I doubted whether this was not too strong meat and only kept it by me in case the spirit should move me to use it as the climax to my speech, otherwise preparing a somewhat milder finish . . . Down to the House . . . But it was not until after eight that I got up in a House of barely a dozen Members. However they streamed in pretty rapidly . . . and I found myself going on to an increasing crescendo of

applause . . . I cast prudence to the winds and ended full out
with my Cromwellian injunction to the Government . . .

Here is the speech's peroration, given in the House of Commons
on 7 May 1940.

Somehow or other we must get into the Government men
who can match our enemies in fighting spirit, in daring, in
resolution and in thirst for victory. Some 300 years ago,
when this House found that its troops were being beaten
again and again by the dash and daring of the Cavaliers, by
Prince Rupert's Cavalry, Oliver Cromwell spoke to John
Hampden. In one of his speeches he recounted what he said.
It was this:

*I said to him, 'Your troops are most of them old, decayed
serving men and tapsters* [publicans] *and such kind of
fellows . . . You must get men of a spirit that are likely to
go as far as they will go, or you will be beaten still.*

It may not be easy to find these men. They can be found
only by trial and by ruthlessly discarding all who fail and
have their failings discovered. We are fighting today for our
life, for our liberty, for our all; we cannot go on being led as
we are. I have quoted certain words of Oliver Cromwell. I
will quote certain other words. I do it with great reluctance,
because I am speaking of those who are old friends and
associates of mine, but they are words which, I think, are
applicable to the present situation. This is what Cromwell
said to the Long Parliament when he thought it was no
longer fit to conduct the affairs of the nation:

*You have sat too long here for any good you have been doing.
Depart, I say, and let us have done with you. In the name of
God, go.*

Note Amery's instinctive grasp of the importance of decorum. He
understood that if the mood wasn't right invoking Cromwell would

do more harm than good, making his criticisms of the government seem exaggerated. The speech's effect was shattering. As Jenkins relates, 'Lloyd George told Amery that it was the most dramatic climax of any speech he had ever heard. And Amery himself thought it helped push the Labour party to force a division at the end of the second day.' That division exposed the Chamberlain government's failing support in the House, and by 6 p.m. on Friday 10 May Winston Churchill was the new prime minister. It just so happened that that very morning Hitler had chosen to end the Phoney War by invading France and the Low Countries. Another dramatic historical turning point offered. Another English public schoolboy soaked in the drama of his country's literature and history was now in charge. What would he say – what could he say – to affect the course of history?

## 5

To find out, let's now go back half a century further in time than Leo Amery dared – to the time of William Shakespeare.

In the spring of 1599, with an English military expedition under the dashing Earl of Essex about to depart to subdue Ireland, Shakespeare hastily completed a new play designed to tap the popular interest in war, *Henry V*. It is far from the playwright's most sophisticated work, but it is among the most dramatic. Having decided to win the French crown by invading France, King Henry V, after a successful siege of Harfleur, is brought to battle against a much larger enemy army at Agincourt. Both battles provide the popularly enduring passages of the play, most notably in two speeches in which Henry rouses his men to the fight. First at Harfleur:

Once more unto the breach, dear friends, once more;
Or close the wall up with our English dead.
In peace there's nothing so becomes a man
As modest stillness and humility:
But when the blast of war blows in our ears,

Then imitate the action of the tiger;
Stiffen the sinews, summon up the blood,
Disguise fair nature with hard-favour'd rage.

Note the similarity of this to Amery's call to find new leaders with the necessary fighting spirit to suit the situation – it's unlikely to be a coincidence.

And then at Agincourt, replying to his lords' complaints about being outnumbered five to one and their wish that more Englishmen were with them:

What's he that wishes so?
My cousin Westmoreland? No, my fair cousin:
If we are mark'd to die, we are enow
To do our country loss; and if to live,
The fewer men, the greater share of honour.
God's will! I pray thee, wish not one man more...
Rather proclaim it, Westmoreland, through my host,
That he which hath no stomach to this fight,
Let him depart; his passport shall be made
And crowns for convoy put into his purse:
We would not die in that man's company
That fears his fellowship to die with us.
This day is called the feast of Crispian:
He that outlives this day, and comes safe home,
Will stand a tip-toe when the day is named,
And rouse him at the name of Crispian.
He that shall live this day, and see old age,
Will yearly on the vigil feast his neighbours,
And say 'To-morrow is Saint Crispian:'
Then will he strip his sleeve and show his scars.
And say 'These wounds I had on Crispin's day.'
Old men forget: yet all shall be forgot,
But he'll remember with advantages
What feats he did that day: then shall our names.
Familiar in his mouth as household words

Harry the king, Bedford and Exeter,
Warwick and Talbot, Salisbury and Gloucester,
Be in their flowing cups freshly remember'd.
This story shall the good man teach his son;
And Crispin Crispian shall ne'er go by,
From this day to the ending of the world,
But we in it shall be remember'd;
We few, we happy few, we band of brothers;
For he to-day that sheds his blood with me
Shall be my brother; be he ne'er so vile,
This day shall gentle his condition:
And gentlemen in England now a-bed
Shall think themselves accursed they were not here,
And hold their manhoods cheap whiles any speaks
That fought with us upon Saint Crispin's day.

In 1944, on the eve of another invasion of France, Lawrence Olivier starred in a movie version of the play. A pilot in the Fleet Air Arm, Olivier wrote later that, 'As I flew over the country in my Walrus [an amphibian aircraft] I kept seeing it as Shakespeare's sceptred isle'. The comment is revealing about the impact of the Bard on the patriotic outlook of Englishmen in the Second World War. Made with just 650 extras wearing silver-painted twine jackets instead of chain mail, and only 160 horsemen made to look like 1000, *Henry V* was the first successful cinematic adaptation of a Shakespeare play, and was a major hit, winning Olivier his first Oscar. Its contemporary relevance was obvious to all: a British army had returned to the continent.

But the play had already made an impact on the war – through the rhetoric of England's new leader, Winston Churchill, who had encouraged Olivier to make the film. A keen student of history, Churchill understood the historical significance of the moment of 1940 and how to use it to motivate men to fight and remember it always. As with Amery and Olivier, his arguments had their origins in the seventeenth century. On 3 June, barely three weeks after he

Olivier as Henry V at Agincourt addresses his band of brothers. Photo: © Getty Images.

became prime minister, the last of the British Expeditionary Force was evacuated from Dunkirk, and France was effectively out of the war. Britain stood alone but together.

Alone, but, like King Harry's outnumbered army, united, determined, a band of brothers, still a force to be reckoned with in the hour of consequence. And one motivated by a very English ideal of patriotism – the small but moated island fortress, the 'sceptred isle' Olivier had seen from the sky, guarded by a happy breed, as described in the prophetic deathbed speech of John of Gaunt in Shakespeare's *King Richard II* (which is one of the most famous literary examples of *asyndeton* and *anaphora* – with thirteen repetitions of 'this' not linked by 'and'):

> This royal throne of kings, this sceptred isle,
> This earth of majesty, this seat of Mars,
> This other Eden, demi-paradise,
> This fortress built by Nature for herself
> Against infection and the hand of war,

This happy breed of men, this little world,
This precious stone set in the silver sea,
Which serves it in the office of a wall
Or as a moat defensive to a house,
Against the envy of less happier lands, –
This blessed plot, this earth, this realm, this England.

In a series of dramatic speeches, Churchill, understanding that the forum of the world looked on, listening with a straining ear, seized his chance as few others have ever done. He succeeded because he combined the rules of rhetorical style, *ethos*, *pathos* and *logos*, with an historian's sense of historical moment, and because he employed *topoi* from the storehouse of English history and drama that had such a deep hold on the English psyche that they were almost guaranteed to create the desired response from the audience. His speeches framed the very way we understand the events of 1940. By contrast, my own country, Australia, besieged, bombed and (so it was widely believed at the time) threatened with invasion in 1942, produced no comparable unifying narrative. What Australia lacked in 1942 was a leader with Churchill's mastery of rhetoric, and a literary tradition capable of stirring the emotions. Only in the 1990s was the significance of Australia's great moment recognised, and only then, in large part, because of the combination of a courageous prime minister, Paul Keating, and his masterful speechwriter – a former historian and playwright no less – Don Watson.

Reading through the most renowned passages of Churchill's speeches from this time, reveals the layering of rhetorical technique and Shakespearean tropes that connected so powerfully with his audience.

Here is the famous line from his first speech as prime minister to the House of Commons on 13 May, which invokes *ethos* through the ideals of courage and sacrifice:

I would say to the House, as I said to those who have joined this government: 'I have nothing to offer but blood, toil, tears and sweat.'

Addressing the House of Commons on 4 June 1940 after the miracle of Dunkirk, Churchill strings together ten successive related clauses, without a single conjunction, to provide a rousing rally to England to fight on against overwhelming odds (it is also perhaps the most remembered example of *anaphora*):

> We shall go on to the end, we shall fight in France, we shall fight on the seas and oceans, we shall fight with growing confidence and growing strength in the air, we shall defend our Island, whatever the cost may be, we shall fight on the beaches, we shall fight on the landing grounds, we shall fight in the fields and in the streets, we shall fight in the hills; we shall never surrender.

A fortnight later, on 18 June, after the formal French surrender, Churchill brilliantly captured the moment by defining the contest as none other than 'the Battle of Britain' itself. Here the Shakespearean *topos* of an island of the brave comes through most strongly – in the claim that Hitler had to 'break us in this island or lose the war' and the idea that (as at Agincourt) the heroism displayed in the coming battle will be remembered for generations to come:

> What General Weygand called the Battle of France is over. I expect that the Battle of Britain is about to begin. Upon this battle depends the survival of Christian civilisation. Upon it depends our own British life, and the long continuity of our institutions and our Empire. The whole fury and might of the enemy must very soon be turned on us. Hitler knows that he will have to break us in this Island or lose the war. If we can stand up to him, all Europe may be free and the life of the world may move forward into broad, sunlit uplands. But if we fail, then the whole world, including the United States, including all that we have known and cared for, will sink into the abyss of a new Dark Age made more sinister, and perhaps more protracted, by the lights of perverted science. Let us therefore brace

ourselves to our duties, and so bear ourselves that, if the British Empire and its Commonwealth last for a thousand years, men will still say, 'This was their finest hour'.

The air battle named in the speech above began on 10 July. Here, in a radio broadcast to the nation on the 14th, Churchill urged his countrymen and women into the breach to fight to the bitter end.

And now it has come to us to stand alone in the breach, and face the worst that the tyrant's might and enmity can do. Bearing ourselves humbly before God, but conscious that we serve an unfolding purpose, we are ready to defend our native land against the invasion by which it is threatened. We are fighting by ourselves alone; but we are not fighting for ourselves alone. Here in this strong City of Refuge which enshrines the title-deeds of human progress and is of deep consequence to Christian civilisation; here, girt about by the seas and oceans where the Navy reigns; shielded from above by the prowess and devotion of our airmen, we await undismayed the impending assault. Perhaps it will come tonight. Perhaps it will come next week. Perhaps it will never come. We must show ourselves equally capable of meeting a sudden violent shock or – what is perhaps a harder test – a prolonged vigil. But be the ordeal sharp or long, or both, we shall seek no terms, we shall tolerate no parley; we may show mercy – we shall ask for none.

On 20 August, with the air battle reaching its height, Churchill paid perhaps his most direct debt to Shakespeare through his re-working of the idea of the 'merry few' and 'band of brothers' to praise the pilots of Fighter Command.

The gratitude of every home in our Island, in our Empire, and indeed throughout the world, except in the abodes of the guilty, goes out to the British airmen who, undaunted by odds, unwearied in their constant challenge and mortal danger, are turning the tide of the world war by their prowess and by their devotion. Never in the field of human conflict was so much owed by so many to so few.

With these historical reference points fixed in the British people's minds, they were left in no doubt that they were living through one of the most vital moments in their nation's life, and were facing the fight of their lives.

# 6

───────────────────────────── 🐾 🐾 🐾 ─────────────────────────────

There are times, though, when the forum itself has to be created. A surging Roman Assembly in the midst of a revolution, a hushed Senate Chamber upon discovery of a coup, a packed House of Commons at a decisive moment of a war, a much-anticipated first inaugural; these are rarities. Even election campaign speeches sometimes need the right backdrop and drama to break into the daily news cycle – in the same way that the visually stunning backdrop to the high-diving board at the Barcelona Olympics made the diving finals so unforgettable. On these occasions the first question the speechwriter asks isn't 'Who is the audience?', but 'What sort of audience do we need?', and 'How do we create it?'

Many of the great speeches mentioned in this book are memorable partly because they created their own forum. Ronald Reagan's famous Pointe du Hoc speech to mark the 40th anniversary of D-Day (which we shall examine in chapter 4) was deliberately staged in front of the German gun emplacements above the cliffs of Pointe du Hoc, to a crowd containing survivors from the Ranger battalion, which had fought that day. Notice how it references its dramatic venue and its audience:

Behind me is a memorial that symbolises the Ranger daggers that were thrust into the top of these cliffs. And before me are the men who put them there. These are the boys of Pointe du Hoc.

Barack Obama's acceptance of the Democratic nomination was made, as we have seen, in front of a reconstruction of the Roman Forum, complete with Styrofoam columns.

Hitler's choreographed demagoguery at Nuremberg provides a more sinister example.

In the early 1960s there was one city guaranteed to provide a forum that would be a magnet for the world's news: Berlin. Since May 1945 it had been the boundary between the two nuclear-armed philosophies of capitalism and communism. This is where Armageddon was expected to begin. It became the setting for three memorable speeches constructed around a common *topos* – Berlin as the city of freedom.

In August 1961 the Soviet-backed East German Government erected the infamous Wall, preventing movement between East and West and raising tensions to a new level. On a visit to Berlin on 26 June 1963 President John F. Kennedy chose the nearby Rudolph Wilde Platz (later re-named John F. Kennedy Platz) fronting the City Hall – the scene of a 300 000-strong demonstration staged after the Wall's construction – to address the people of Berlin. Kennedy's speechwriter, Ted Sorensen, describes the stage they created:

> It was a beautiful day and the largest, most enthusiastic
> crowd I had ever seen. As I stood behind JFK on the city hall
> steps . . . I looked out on a vast area totally carpeted with
> people in every direction, filling every window of every
> building on the square, not far from that offense against
> humanity known as the Berlin Wall.

The speech, delivered from notes on cards, was a combination of thoughtful drafting by Sorensen, with additions Kennedy made himself on the flight into Berlin, helped by the German-speaking national security adviser McGeorge Bundy. It is a masterpiece of classical rhetorical technique, from the perfect balance of the first paragraph below, to the *anaphora* and *epiphora* of the second, to the distillation of the concept of *ethos* in the Latin boast '*civis Romanus sum*'. But it is the subject matter of the poetry, not just its form, that ensured Kennedy's success – the heroism of the host city and its people, and the proximity of the world's ultimate stage prop, the Berlin Wall.

Two thousand years ago the proudest boast was *civis Romanus sum*. Today, in the world of freedom, the proudest boast is *Ich bin ein Berliner . . .*

There are many people in the world who really don't understand, or say they don't, what is the great issue between the free world and the communist world. Let them come to Berlin. There are some who say that communism is the wave of the future. Let them come to Berlin. And there are some who say in Europe and elsewhere we can work with the communists. Let *them* come to Berlin. And there are even a few who say that it is true that communism is an evil system, but it permits us to make economic progress. *Lass' sie nach Berlin kommen*. Let them come to Berlin.

Freedom has many difficulties and democracy is not perfect, but we have never had to put a wall up to keep our people in, to prevent them from leaving us. I want to say, on behalf of my countrymen, who live many miles away on the other side of the Atlantic, who are far distant from you, that they take the greatest pride that they have been able to share with you, even from a distance, the story of the last 18 years. I know of no town, no city, that has been besieged for 18 years that still lives with the vitality and the force, and the hope and the determination of the city of West Berlin. While the wall is the most obvious and vivid demonstration of the failures of the communist system, for all the world to see, we take no satisfaction in it, for it is, as your Mayor has said, an offense not only against history but an offense against humanity, separating families, dividing husbands and wives and brothers and sisters, and dividing a people who wish to be joined together . . .

Freedom is indivisible, and when one man is enslaved, all are not free. When all are free, then we can look forward to that day when this city will be joined as one and this country and this great Continent of Europe is a peaceful and hopeful globe. When that day finally comes, as it will, the people of West Berlin can take sober satisfaction in the fact that they were in the front lines for almost two decades.

All free men, wherever they may live, are citizens of Berlin, and, therefore, as a free man, I take pride in the words *Ich bin ein Berliner*.

Ever since the speech, an inconclusive debate has raged around whether or not the inclusion of the indefinite article *ein* in *Ich bin ein Berliner* meant that Kennedy had inadvertently referred to himself as a type of jelly doughnut (called 'a Berliner') then popular in that city. Whatever the case, the claims demonstrate that, like a blemish on an otherwise perfect face, a minor fault can add to a speech's beauty. Of more substance was the criticism that – with two armies facing each other across Checkpoint Charlie – the speech's implied argument that East and West could not work together and that the West must triumph, was inflammatory. In such conditions, words were potentially not bullets but intercontinental ballistic missiles. In response to his worried foreign policy advisers, Kennedy adopted a more conciliatory tone in a speech later that day. But he was right to have allowed himself to be carried away by democratic principle. This was not just because no conflict ever resulted from it, or because the words were so cheering to the crowd that the ovation lasted for 15 minutes, but because the successful example it set encouraged another president a quarter of a century later to return to Berlin and make a speech that contributed more directly to achieving Kennedy's goal of toppling the wall and uniting the two opposing civilisations.

# 7

Ronald Reagan may not have been an intellectual's idea of a great president, but he possessed the principled man's moral clarity and the actor's understanding of the power of words and their effective delivery. He needed them, because in the State Department and even his own White House he was up against two of the most obfuscating, passive language generating machines that bureaucracy has ever created. Peggy Noonan frequently railed against their interference in the President's speeches, and, mockingly, pondered what they would have said about some of the most famous speeches in American history, including *Ich bin ein Berliner* ('The President isn't from Berlin and everyone knows it.').

Despite the success of John F. Kennedy's Berlin speech, the proposal by Reagan's speechwriting team, led now by Antony Dolan, for the President to exhort the Soviets to tear down the Wall, was tenaciously opposed by the foreign policy and political establishment, up to and including Secretary of State Colin Powell – using the same arguments they had made against Kennedy in 1963. How the speechwriters got the speech onto the President's lectern – by a series of bureaucratic feints, getting Reagan himself to own it, and then fighting their opponents to a standstill – illustrates one of the practical lessons all speechwriters must learn: you are the speech; it's your job to protect it from the ruinous interference of the literal minded, detail freaks and policy obsessives on your staff; and your job doesn't end with the writing; it only ends when your words appear with favourable comment on the front page of the next morning's newspapers. Speechwriters' filing cabinets are full with unfamous and undelivered but – in their authors' humble opinion – great speeches.

Like Kennedy's Berlin address, Reagan's represented the triumph of speech over politics. In 1963 the recently built Wall represented a dramatic reference point for a presidential speech; in 1987 new East–West tensions over the deployment of medium-range nuclear missiles had given a Berlin speech its own contemporary significance. Reagan chose the Wall itself as the highly televisual backdrop, and the speech itself was broadcast over loudspeakers across no man's land to East Berlin. In it one can hear intentional echoes of Kennedy's style and arguments, most notably its direct references to the physical forum of the city and the courage of its people, the way it used the German language (*Ich hab' noch einen Koffer in Berlin*), and its argument that freedom is indivisible and its absence in East Berlin is an affront to humanity ('every man is a German . . . every man is a Berliner'). In following Kennedy in this way, Reagan was using tried and tested *topoi* that were almost certain to appeal to his audience.

The confidence that this would work was added to because the speech was also built on something indispensible to any great speech (and which provides another practical lesson for the budding speechwriter) – real knowledge of the views of the audience members gathered by good reconnaissance. As we will see in chapter 5, the devastating and election-winning line of Australian Prime Minister John Howard in 2001 – '*We* will decide who comes to this country and the circumstances in which they come'– was lifted from a focus group conducted by conservative pollsters; it was the same in this case. As historian Robert Schlesinger recounts, doubting the assertion then doing the rounds that discussion of the Wall was passé to a new generation, White House speechwriter Peter Robinson travelled to Berlin and listened to the dinner party conversation of typical Berliners. Amid the recounting of stories about separated families and other humiliations, one woman 'pounded her fist into her open palm' and said, 'If this man Gorbachev is serious with his talk about *glasnost* and *perestroika*, he can prove it. He can get rid of this wall'. Robinson had his line! With all the elements of forum present – tension, backdrop, audience connection – Reagan

Ronald Reagan uses words to bring walls crashing down. Photo:
© Time & Life Pictures/Getty Images.

had the makings of a truly memorable speech. When he stepped up
to the purpose-built rostrum overlooking the Wall on 12 June 1987
its message was rammed home by the masterful use of *apostrophe*
(directly addressing someone other than the immediate audience)
and by superb delivery, which milked the moment for not one but
two bursts of applause. (Reagan's own handwritten emphases are
included in the last paragraph of the transcript.) Notice the use the
speech makes of its backdrop, the Wall, and of Kennedy's famous
Berlin oration:

> Twenty-four years ago, President John F. Kennedy visited
> Berlin, speaking to the people of this city and the world at

the City Hall. Well, since then two other presidents have come, each in his turn, to Berlin. And today I, myself, make my second visit to your city.

We come to Berlin, we American presidents, because it's our duty to speak, in this place, of freedom. But I must confess, we're drawn here by other things as well: by the feeling of history in this city, more than 500 years older than our own nation; by the beauty of the Grunewald and the Tiergarten; most of all, by your courage and determination. Perhaps the composer Paul Lincke understood something about American presidents. You see, like so many presidents before me, I come here today because wherever I go, whatever I do: *Ich hab' noch einen Koffer in Berlin.* [I still have a suitcase in Berlin.]

Our gathering today is being broadcast throughout Western Europe and North America. I understand that it is being seen and heard as well in the East. To those listening throughout Eastern Europe, a special word: Although I cannot be with you, I address my remarks to you just as surely as to those standing here before me. For I join you, as I join your fellow countrymen in the West, in this firm, this unalterable belief: *Es gibt nur ein Berlin.* [There is only one Berlin.]

Behind me stands a wall that encircles the free sectors of this city, part of a vast system of barriers that divides the entire continent of Europe. From the Baltic, south, those barriers cut across Germany in a gash of barbed wire, concrete, dog runs, and guard towers. Farther south, there may be no visible, no obvious wall. But there remain armed guards and checkpoints all the same – still a restriction on the right to travel, still an instrument to impose upon ordinary men and women the will of a totalitarian state. Yet it is here in Berlin where the wall emerges most clearly; here, cutting across your city, where the news photo and the television screen have imprinted this brutal division of a continent upon the mind of the world. Standing before the Brandenburg Gate, every man is a German, separated from his fellow men. Every man is a Berliner, forced to look upon a scar.

President von Weizsacker has said, 'The German question is open as long as the Brandenburg Gate is closed'. Today I say: As long as the gate is closed, as long as this scar of a wall is permitted to stand, it is not the German question alone that remains open, but the question of freedom for all mankind . . .

And now the Soviets themselves may, in a limited way, be coming to understand the importance of freedom. We hear much from Moscow about a new policy of reform and openness. Some political prisoners have been released. Certain foreign news broadcasts are no longer being jammed. Some economic enterprises have been permitted to operate with greater freedom from state control.

Are these the beginnings of profound changes in the Soviet state? Or are they token gestures, intended to raise false hopes in the West, or to strengthen the Soviet system without changing it? We welcome change and openness; for we believe that freedom and security go together, that the advance of human liberty can only strengthen the cause of world peace. There is one sign the Soviets can make that would be unmistakable, that would advance dramatically the cause of freedom and peace.

General Secretary Gorbachev, if you seek peace, ///
if you seek prosperity for the Soviet Union and Eastern
Europe, /// if you seek liberalization: ///

Come here to this gate! Mr. Gorbachev, open this gate! ///
[APPLAUSE] /// Mr. Gorbachev, tear down this wall!
[APPLAUSE]

What direct part Reagan's speeches played in ending the Cold War
will be long debated by historians, but it's likely that by ignoring
the bureaucrats, sticking to his principles, and insisting on delivering memorable speeches, Reagan helped keep the pressure on
the Soviet reformers. Two-and-a-half years later the Berlin Wall
fell, and not long after, the former President had the satisfaction of
knocking a small part of it down himself – perhaps for the second
time.

# 8

After winning the primary race, Barack Obama turned his attention to the presidential election. Appealing to Democratic activists
and supporters had been the easy part; after all, Obama's very candidacy, combined with his ability to project idealism through his
oratory, was a vindication of the primary voters' own liberalism.
Now he had to convince Democrats and Republicans alike that
he wasn't just another flip-flopping liberal but someone with the
gravitas and strength to represent the nation and be Commander in
Chief. His problem was obvious. He had little foreign policy experience and no military record, whereas John McCain's was outstand-
ing. So in late July 2008 his campaign team organised a ten-day,
eight-country international tour designed to project his grasp of
world affairs. And where else would an American politician go to
get a rapturous reception and a forum of international significance
but . . . Berlin?

The Berlin Wall may have come down nearly two decades prior,
but it still remained the focus of Obama's speech, made on 24 July
2008, to the largest audience of his campaign so far, close to where
the Wall had stood in front of the Victory Column (itself a classical
architectural backdrop topped by Victoria, the goddess of victory,

whose original temple had stood on the Palatine overlooking the same Forum where Cicero once spoke).

The speech's debt to the messages of Kennedy and Reagan was implicit. By surviving the Berlin Airlift and by tearing down the Wall, the people of Berlin had done their duty and set the standard for the citizens of the world to emulate in the struggles that faced a new generation. It built to this *climax*, which drew upon biblical imagery of walls tumbling down:

> Sixty years after the airlift, we are called upon again. History has led us to a new crossroad, with new promise and new peril. When you, the German people, tore down that wall – a wall that divided East and West, freedom and tyranny, fear and hope – walls came tumbling down around the world. From Kiev to Cape Town, prison camps were closed, and the doors of democracy were opened. Markets opened too, and the spread of information and technology reduced barriers to opportunity and prosperity. While the 20th century taught us that we share a common destiny, the 21st has revealed a world more intertwined than at any time in human history.

> The fall of the Berlin Wall brought new hope. But that very closeness has given rise to new dangers – dangers that cannot be contained within the borders of a country or by the distance of an ocean.

> The terrorists of September 11th plotted in Hamburg and trained in Kandahar and Karachi before killing thousands from all over the globe on American soil.

> As we speak, cars in Boston and factories in Beijing are melting the ice caps in the Arctic, shrinking coastlines in the Atlantic, and bringing drought to farms from Kansas to Kenya.

Poorly secured nuclear material in the former Soviet Union, or secrets from a scientist in Pakistan could help build a bomb that detonates in Paris. The poppies in Afghanistan become the heroin in Berlin. The poverty and violence in Somalia breeds the terror of tomorrow. The genocide in Darfur shames the conscience of us all.

In this new world, such dangerous currents have swept along faster than our efforts to contain them. That is why we cannot afford to be divided. No one nation, no matter how large or powerful, can defeat such challenges alone. None of us can deny these threats, or escape responsibility in meeting them. Yet, in the absence of Soviet tanks and a terrible wall, it has become easy to forget this truth. And if we're honest with each other, we know that sometimes, on both sides of the Atlantic, we have drifted apart, and forgotten our shared destiny . . .

That is why the greatest danger of all is to allow new walls to divide us from one another. The walls between old allies on either side of the Atlantic cannot stand. The walls between the countries with the most and those with the least cannot stand. The walls between races and tribes; natives and immigrants, Christian and Muslim and Jew cannot stand. These now are the walls we must tear down.

Meanwhile, on the other side of the Atlantic, Obama's opponent, John McCain, was travelling the country by bus, addressing small audiences of listless, ageing Republican diehards, in community centres remarkable only for their ordinariness. His forum had already melted away.

## 9

Most speechwriters, armed with the skills of their trade and the experience necessary to employ them effectively, are capable of producing a great speech – on paper at least. What they also need is the luck to be at the top of their game when a gifted orator emerges to confront an important moment in history. It's when these three features – speechwriter, politician and moment – coincide that the truly great speeches are created. A forum has been created, won and held.

Now it's time to examine the question of how the orator *holds* the forum.

# Chapter 4
# **Style**

## 1

Near the conclusion of his dramatic speech over Caesar's body, Shakespeare's Antony delivers these intriguing lines:

> I am no orator, as Brutus is;
> But, as you know me all, a plain blunt man,
> That love my friend . . .

Why such modesty and praise for the competition? You wouldn't want it from your surgeon mid-incision: 'That other surgeon – the one your health fund *wouldn't* pay for – he's far more skilled than I am.' Cicero knew:

> *Propeterea quod prudentia hominibus grata est, lingua suspecta.*
> The reason is that practical knowledge is pleasing to men, but a clever tongue is suspect.

Fine oratory, we fear, is a trick to overwhelm the listener's reason and camouflage poor logic and weak evidence. But it works. In fact, denying eloquence is part of the trick, and those who deny eloquence loudest are often those who employ it most effectively.

So just how 'plain' and 'blunt' was Antony'?

## 2
———————————— ❧ ❧ ❧ ————————————

The earliest rhetoricians understood that the brain had its own ways of arranging speech to make it more appealing to the mind, tongue and ear – punctuation divided speech into clauses, sentences and paragraphs to separate out ideas and coordinate reading and breathing. They also realised that the way words were used and arranged in speech could alter their meaning and force. The genius of Aristotle, Cicero and Quintilian developed these insights into a system of technical classification that helps us understand why politicians speak the way they do. Some of their terms are still in common usage, such as euphemism, hyperbole, climax, anticlimax, alliteration and sarcasm. But while we may no longer be taught any other of these classifications by name (as Shakespeare was), we are all familiar with their effects. It's what we mean when we recognise that someone is speaking figuratively.

The classical theorists divided these figures into two categories:

- *tropes* – changes in the normally accepted meaning of the words, often involving the use of metaphors
- *schemes* – calculated differences in the way words are arranged to make them more attractive or give them greater force.

There are thousands of tropes and schemes that would require a lifetime to memorise. Here we look at some of the most common to see their importance to great speeches. A list of these tropes and schemes is included in Appendix 1. Shakespeare used them to good effect, as the duel between Brutus and Antony demonstrates.

Here's Brutus, whom Antony (accurately as this will show) backhandedly complimented as a foppish, fanciful, oratorical stylist. Tropes have a white background; schemes have a grey one.

## Tropes and schemes between Brutus and Antony

| | |
|---|---|
| Romans, countrymen, and lovers! | *tricolon*: Brutus uses a series of three to emphasise points – in this case to address the audience |
| ...hear me for my cause, and be silent, that you may hear: believe me for mine honour, and have respect to mine honour, that you may believe: | *epanalepsis*: he begins and ends clauses with the same words – 'hear' and 'believe' *epiphora*: he ends successive clauses with the same words – 'mine honour' *parallelism*: each sentence has similar construction – each of the three sentences has three clauses (two major and one subordinate), making it a highly sophisticated tricolon |
| censure me in your wisdom, and awake your senses, that you may the better judge | *antithesis*: he juxtaposes contrasting ideas of censuring and judging |
| If there be any in this assembly, any dear friend of Caesar's, to him I say, that Brutus' love to Caesar was no less than his. If then that friend demand why Brutus rose against Caesar, this is my answer: – Not that I loved Caesar less, but that I loved Rome more. | *anaphora*: he repeats a word that begins successive sentences or clauses – 'if' and 'that I loved' *ratiocination*: Brutus states a position, questions it, and then answers it himself *antithesis*: he juxtaposes 'not loved Caesar less' and 'loved Rome more' *paradox*: he poses a supposed contradiction (that although he loved Caesar he killed him) to evoke a truth (that Brutus is a patriot) |
| Had you rather Caesar were living and die all slaves, than that Caesar were dead, to live all free men? | *erotema*: Brutus asks a rhetorical question *antithesis*: juxtaposition of life and death, slavery and freedom |

**Tropes and schemes between Brutus and Antony (*cont.*)**

| | |
|---|---|
| As Caesar loved me, I weep for him; as he was fortunate, I rejoice at it; as he was valiant, I honour him: but, as he was ambitious, I slew him. | *anaphora*: repetition at the start of successive clauses of 'as' and 'I' *epiphora*: repetition of 'him' at the end of successive clauses *symploce*: the combination of anaphora and epiphora in the same sentence *accumulation*: Brutus' argument is summarised in a forceful manner |
| There is tears for his love; joy for his fortune; honour for his valour; and death for his ambition. | *climax*: the consequences of Caesar's virtues and flaws are listed in rising order of importance – 'tears', 'joy', honour' and 'ambition' *parallelism*: each clause is similarly constructed around 'for his' |
| Who is here so base that would be a bondman? If any, speak; for him have I offended. Who is here so rude that would not be a Roman? If any, speak; for him have I offended. Who is here so vile that will not love his country? If any, speak; for him have I offended. I pause for a reply. ALL: None, Brutus, none. BRUTUS: Then none have I offended. | *pysma*: Brutus asks multiple rhetorical questions (in fact, three, making this a tricolon) *anaphora*: repetition of 'who' and 'if' at the beginning of sentences. *epiphora*: repetition of second sentence *epitrope*: Brutus turns the answer over to his audience |

Shakespeare used this speech to display his grammar-school grasp of classical rhetoric, but in a way that satirises the sort of class-room declamation exercises the more educated Elizabethan audience members would, probably painfully, remember (resembling the well-known scene from the Monty Python movie *The Life of Brian* in which a Roman centurion forces Brian to decline and conjugate the Latin slogans he'd just daubed on the city walls). It's the type of showing off that Gorgias liked and Cicero despised, and it serves to make Brutus seem prim, aloof and slightly ridiculous.

But what of Antony? We will investigate other aspects of his reply elsewhere, but let's continue the passage which opened this chapter. Plain? Blunt?

## Tropes and schemes between Brutus and Antony (*cont.*)

| | |
|---|---|
| I am no orator, as Brutus is;<br>But, as you know me all, a plain<br>  blunt man,<br>That love my friend; and that<br>  they know full well<br>That gave me public leave to<br>  speak of him: | *irony*: Brutus is saying one thing<br>  but is proving he's in fact<br>  doing the other<br>*empathy*: he is also creating a<br>  bond with the audience<br>*commiseration*: he is invoking pity<br>  because he's lost his friend |
| For I have neither wit, nor words,<br>  nor worth,<br>Action, nor utterance, nor the<br>  power of speech,<br>To stir men's blood: | *polysyndeton*: he repeats<br>  conjunctions for poetic effect –<br>  'nor'<br>*irony:* he couldn't be more<br>  eloquent |
| I only speak right on;<br>I tell you that which you<br>  yourselves do know; | *irony*: he's doing it again |
| Show you sweet Caesar's<br>  wounds, poor poor dumb<br>  mouths, | *personification*: he ascribes<br>  agency to inanimate objects –<br>  Caesar's wounds speak |
| And bid them speak for me:<br>but were I Brutus,<br>And Brutus Antony, there were<br>  an Antony<br>Would ruffle up your spirits and<br>  put a tongue<br>In every wound of Caesar that<br>  should move<br>The stones of Rome to rise and<br>  mutiny. | *irony*: Antony ascribes to Brutus<br>  what he himself is actually<br>  doing<br>*personification*: Caesar's wounds<br>  speak and stones revolt<br>*hyperbole*: he is exaggerating to<br>  provide emphasis – in this case<br>  Brutus' reputation as a<br>  silver-tongued orator |

Shakespeare demonstrates how even those who play the 'plain blunt' speaker can use rhetorical technique to obtain their ends.

Look again at the right-hand columns of Brutus' and Antony's speeches. They tell us something significant about the way the two orators have approached their tasks: the predominantly grey panels of Brutus' text shows he has concentrated on *schemes* or word arrangement to win over his audience; Antony's predominantly white-backed text shows he has concentrated on *tropes* or altering the meaning of words – something that denotes a more ruthless, less transparent, less democratic approach to winning the debate.

## 3

While few now know the technical names for these figures of speech, we actually hear them from politicians every day when we watch the evening news: using the same word with double meaning; employing overstatement and understatement; asking a question and sometimes answering it; balancing a statement with its opposite; using the same words but in a different order; and repeating words, clauses and sounds. Watch a good or even moderate speaker in a political meeting or on television and you will notice that the applause tends to follow the use of these rhetorical devices. It's as if audience members know instinctively when the speaker wants them to clap and cheer and boo and chant and chorus a reply.

Used amateurishly and obviously, the speechwriter's tools can distract the listener from the substance of what is being said. But used well, they can attract the ear without audience members realising why. Cicero again has it:

> the decision as to subject matter and words to express it belongs to the intellect, but in the choice of sounds and rhythms the ear is the judge; the former are dependent on the understanding, the latter on pleasure; therefore reason determines the rules of art in the former case, and sensation in the latter. We had thus either to neglect the favour of those whom we were striving to please, or find some art of winning it.

(Or listen to your opponent winning it instead.) This means that style should not be dismissed as frippery – as it is by many journalistic critics of orating. As Cicero puts it, 'The significance of style is not so much to add colour to language as to present ideas with increased vividness to make the speaker's case more convincing'.

Figures of speech are in fact the building blocks of something we all know: the sound bite. Some argue that the sound bite – that part of a speech written to stand out and be quoted by the media – is a modern contrivance that has undermined oratory. Why bother to give a well-crafted speech when only one line from it will be quoted? (Anyone who has ever worked in a busy political office will tell you that sometimes the bite is all there's time to produce and all that harried, time-poor newsroom producers will replay.) But as Ronald Reagan's famous speechwriter Peggy Noonan points out, 'The sound bite has been a feature of speech from the very beginnings of oratory; it is simply the line in the speech we remember most'. In fact, re-read in full, the so-called great speeches can sometimes seem rather disappointing; but they invariably contain a memorable figure of speech, which a Cicero would have recognised.

The lesson for the speechwriter is obvious: if you want to write a great or even good speech, it pays to put time, effort or inspiration into getting the sound bite right. The question should be: which line do I want the audience members, the television viewers, the radio listeners and the newspaper readers to remember and repeat? One of the secrets to producing a memorable sound bite is the use of figures of speech.

Let's look at some examples of the most common figures of speech and how they have given life to great speeches.

**Alliteration:** *commencing closely connected words with the same letter or sound*

In the early hours of Sunday 31 August 1997, Diana, Princess of Wales, was killed in a car crash in Paris. It was to be a big moment for the young new Prime Minister Tony Blair. As his press secretary Alistair Campbell recounted in his diary, Blair understood that this would lead to an unprecedented outpouring of grief, in a way that

The young Tony Blair – orator in the grand style. Photo: © Getty Images.

even the death of the Queen would not, and would be a tricky
moment that would help frame the new government's image.

> It was pretty emotional. TB was genuinely shocked. It was
> also going to be a big test for him, the first time in which the
> country had looked to him in a moment of shock and grief.
> We went round and round in circles about what he should
> say, and also how . . . Just after seven TB called again. He'd
> been working on the words for his doorstop at the church
> and he was going over some lines he'd drafted. We agreed
> that it was fine to be emotional, and to call her the People's
> Princess. It was a very powerful piece of communication.
> The People's Princess was very easily the strongest line and
> the people in the studio afterwards were clearly impressed,
> and felt he had really caught the mood.

The reason was, in part, because it was a memorable piece of alliteration (preceded by a nice *symploce* and *tricolon*).

> People everywhere, not just here in Britain, kept faith with
> Princess Diana. They liked her, they loved her, they
> regarded her as one of the people. She was the People's

Princess and that is how she will stay, how she will remain in our hearts and our memories forever.

**Anadiplosis:** *the repetition of the last word or words of a clause at the start of the following clause.*

Here's Barack Obama delivering his stump speech (a stock speech containing the speaker's main messages, delivered multiple times, usually on the campaign trail) at the very last rally of his presidential campaign, at Prince William County Fairground in Manassas, Virginia, 3 November 2008, with a classic example of *anadiplosis*:

> One voice can change a room, and if one voice can change a room, then it can change a city, and if it can change a city, it can change a state, and if it can change a state, it can change a nation, and if it can change a nation, it can change the world. Come on, Virginia, let's go change the world!

**Anaphora:** *repetition of a word or phrase at the beginning of successive clauses or sentences*

One of the most famous examples of *anaphora* is the Beatitudes from the Sermon on the Mount, in which Jesus begins nine successive sentences with 'blessed' and seven successive subordinate clauses with 'for':

> And seeing the multitudes, he went up into a mountain: and when he was set, his disciples came unto him: and he opened his mouth, and taught them, saying, Blessed are the poor in spirit: for theirs is the kingdom of heaven. Blessed are they that mourn: for they shall be comforted. Blessed are the meek: for they shall inherit the earth. Blessed are they which do hunger and thirst after righteousness: for they shall be filled. Blessed are the merciful: for they shall obtain mercy. Blessed are the pure in heart: for they shall see God. Blessed are the peacemakers: for they shall be called the children of God. Blessed are they which are persecuted for righteousness' sake: for theirs is the kingdom of heaven.

Blessed are ye, when men shall revile you, and persecute
you, and shall say all manner of evil against you falsely, for
my sake.

**Anthimeria:** *the substitution of one part of speech for another (e.g.
nouns as verbs, nouns as adjectives, etc.)*

In his first inaugural address on 4 March 1933, Franklin D. Roosevelt
projected confidence and purposefulness by using 'fear' as a verb
and noun.

The only thing we have to fear is fear itself – nameless,
unreasoning, unjustified terror which paralyses needed
efforts to convert retreat into advance.

**Antimetabole**: *repetition of words in successive clauses but in (rough)
reverse order*

In his inaugural address of 20 January 1961, John F. Kennedy
inverted (roughly) 'Ask not what your country can do for you'
to call for a new era of idealism and sacrifice for the common good.
Ted Sorensen called this technique 'the reversible raincoat' – like
Graham Freudenberg in chapter 2, Sorensen only later became
aware that he was indulging in classical rhetorical technique.

And so, my fellow Americans, ask not what your country
can do for you; ask what you can do for your country.

**Antithesis**: *the employment of opposite or contrasting ideas*

On Monday 20 April 1962, the leader of the ANC Nelson Mandela
got to his feet in a Johannesburg courtroom to read a statement that
opened his defence in his trial for treason – for which he expected
the death penalty. He used the occasion to good effect, with a
speech rich in figurative language, including a memorable use of
*antithesis* that pits life against death.

During my lifetime I have dedicated myself to this struggle
of the African people. I have fought against white
domination, and I have fought against black domination.

I have cherished the ideal of a democratic and free society in which all persons live together in harmony and with equal opportunities. It is an ideal which I hope to live for and achieve. But if needs be, it is an ideal for which I am prepared to die.

**Asyndeton:** *the omission of conjunctions between words or clauses*

In the crucial scene from the 2000 epic Hollywood movie *Gladiator*, the former general and now swordfighter, Maximus Decimus Meridius, played by Australian actor Russell Crowe, having just despatched his opponents in the Coliseum, is ordered by the usurping Emperor Commodus to remove his helmet and show his identity. His response provides the most remembered scene from the movie and the one that sums up its story, revenge. But it almost never made it into the film. The screenplay, which went through a number of iterations, had to overcome one last-minute obstacle when Crowe, who hated the dialogue and had fought the director to have it altered, at first refused to say the line. As the screenwriter Bill Nicholson relates, Crowe told him: 'Your lines are garbage but I'm the greatest actor in the world, and I can make even garbage sound good'. Crowe *was* a brilliant actor, but he was wrong about the script; it was a great line – and what made it great was its combination of *ethos* and *asyndeton*.

> My name is Maximus Decimus Meridius, Commander of the Armies of the North, General of the Felix Legions, loyal servant to the true emperor, Marcus Aurelius; father to a murdered son, husband to a murdered wife. And I will have my vengeance, in this life or the next.

**Epiphora**: *repetition of a word or set of words at the end of a clause or sentence*

For *epiphora* we need look no further than the *Ich bin ein Berliner* speech by John F. Kennedy, provided in chapter 3. Such was the sophistication of Kennedy's and his speechwriter Sorensen's use of the technique of end repetition that the catch phrase 'let them come to Berlin' was repeated five times, including the fourth time in German as *Lass' sie nach Berlin kommen*.

**Erotema**: *asking a rhetorical question*
**Pysma**: *asking multiple rhetorical questions*
**Anthypophora**: *the speaker immediately answers the question*

Addressing the Labour Party Conference in Llandudno in Wales on 15 May 1987 in the lead up to that year's general election, its leader, Neil Kinnock, who, like Barack Obama won the leadership of his party by being its best orator, denounced the Thatcher government by exploiting the potential of the rhetorical question. In this passage, made famous when it was copied by Senator Joe Biden during the presidential primary campaign the following year, he asks no fewer than a dozen questions and provides a powerful answer to them all. (Note also its liberal use of *symploce, asyndeton* and *polysyndeton*.)

> Why am I the first Kinnock in a thousand generations to be able to get to university? Why is Glenys [his wife] the first woman in her family in a thousand generations to be able to get to university? Was it because all our predecessors were thick? Did they lack talent – those people who could sing and play, and recite and write poetry; those people who could make wonderful, beautiful things with their hands; those people who could dream dreams, see visions; those people who had such a sense of perception as to know in times so brutal, so oppressive, that they could win their way out of that by coming together? Were those people not university material? Couldn't they have knocked off their A Levels in an afternoon? But why didn't they get it? Was it because they were weak – those people who could work eight hours underground and then come up and play football? Weak? Those women who could survive eleven childbearings, were *they* weak? Those people who could

Neil Kinnock – the man with the questions. Photo: © David Fowler/
Shutterstock.com.

stand with their backs and their legs straight and face the
great – the people who had control over their lives, the ones
that owned the workplaces and tried to own them – and tell
them: 'No I won't take your orders'. Were *they* weak? Does
anyone really think that they didn't get what we had
because they didn't have the talent, or the strength, or the
endurance, or the commitment? Of course not. It was
because there was no platform on which they could stand.

**Exuscitatio**: *using rhetorical questions to inflame the audience's
passions*

Howard Dean made a dramatic entry into national US politics in
2003 by inciting a grass roots populist campaign for the Democratic
presidential nomination. His primary campaign was given momentum by an extraordinary speech to the California State Democratic Convention on 15 March 2003, which was based around
five inflammatory questions rank-and-file party members wanted
answered. Here is how the speech opened. (Its questions are also
*anaphora*, and its ending – 'I'm here to represent the Democratic

wing of the Democratic Party' – is a form of *paronomasia*, which turns a proper noun into an adjective.)

> What I want to know is what in the world so many Democrats are doing supporting the President's unilateral intervention in Iraq? [APPLAUSE]

> What I want to know is what in the world so many Democrats are doing supporting tax cuts, which have bankrupted this country and given us the largest deficit in the history of the United States? [APPLAUSE]

> What I want to know is why the Congress is fighting over the Patient's Bill of Rights? The Patient's Bill of Rights is a good bill, but not one more person gets health insurance and it's not 5 cents cheaper. [APPLAUSE]

> What I want to know is why the Democrats in Congress aren't standing up for us, joining every other industrialised country on the face of the Earth in providing health insurance for every man, woman and child in America. [APPLAUSE]

> What I want to know is why so many folks in Congress are voting for the President's Education Bill– 'The No School Board Left Standing Bill'– the largest unfunded mandate in the history of our educational system! [APPLAUSE]...

> I am Howard Dean, and I'm here to represent the Democratic wing of the Democratic Party. [CHEERS, APPLAUSE]

**Hyperbole**: *intentional exaggeration not meant to be taken literally*

As we shall see elsewhere in this book, race is a vexed topic for orators, usually producing bitter controversy. One person who rejoiced in controversy was the British MP Enoch Powell. A man of extraordinary intellect and ability, who obtained a double-starred first at Cambridge, became a classics professor at the age of twenty-five (teaching, among others, the Roman-like orator, Australian Prime

Minister Gough Whitlam) and rose from private to brigadier during the Second World War, Powell lacked the statesman-like virtues of tolerance and tact. In a speech that ended his frontbench career, Powell denounced the Race Relations Act and, by extension, non-white migration to Britain. With its calls for the end of so-called special privileges for immigrants, equality before the law for whites, and for re-immigration to source countries, it has become a model for anti-immigrant populists the world over, and echoes can be heard in the 'fish-and-chip shop lady' speech by the Australian dem-agogue Pauline Hanson (discussed in chapter 8). Made on 20 April 1968 (just three weeks after Martin Luther King's 'Mountaintop' speech and assassination and Bobby Kennedy's famous response – discussed in chapter 5) Powell's speech predicts the consequences of immigration through an indirect reference to the Sibyl prophesies in the *Aeneid*, making this an example also of *allusion*:

> As I look ahead, I am filled with foreboding; like the Roman,
> I seem to see 'the River Tiber foaming with much blood'.

**Polysyndeton**: *the repetition of conjunctions between related clauses*

At the British Labour Party's 1960 conference in Scarborough, its leader Hugh Gaitskell lost his fight to prevent the party adopting a policy of unilateral nuclear disarmament and was expected to resign. But he managed to steal the moment for history. Minutes before the vote was taken he made a dramatic speech remembered for its political courage but also its use of *polysyndeton* (and *epiphora* and *alliteration* and *tricolon*).

> There are some of us, Mr Chairman, who will fight, and
> fight, and fight again, to save the party we love. We will
> fight, and fight, and fight again, to bring back sanity and
> honesty and dignity, so that our party – with its great past –
> may retain its glory and its greatness.

**Parison**: *each clause or sentence has a similar construction*
**Isocolon**: *the construction of each clause is exactly alike*

Winston Churchill, as we have already seen, was a master of rhetorical style. His chief opponent also understood the power of using figures of speech. Adolf Hitler's stump speech usually contained the following *parison*. Each of the three clauses (therefore making it a *tricolon*) has two words and starts with an 'ein' (making it also an example of *anaphora*), and its lack of conjunctions makes it an example of *asyndeton*.

> *Ein volk, ein reich, ein Führer.*
> One people, one state, one leader.

**Paronomasia**: *a pun, using similar sounding words with differing meanings*

Margaret Thatcher defines her prime ministership with a show-stealing catchphrase. Photo: © David Fowler/Shutterstock.com.

At the Conservative Party Conference on 10 October 1980, countering calls from inside and outside her own party to reverse her anti-inflationary policy in the face of recession and rising unemployment, Margaret Thatcher famously punned on the common phrase 'U-turn'. The line was written by her speechwriter

Ronnie Millar. In the delivered version the last, unexpected sentence (which comprises a subtle *epanalepsis*) is delayed by strong laughter and applause, making its delivery a show stealer. It was one of the defining moments of Thatcher's career.

> To those waiting with bated breath for that favourite media catchphrase, the U-turn, I have only one thing to say: 'You turn if you want to. [APPLAUSE] The lady's not for turning'.

**Symploce**: *the combination of* anaphora *and* epiphora

As a young shadow home secretary Tony Blair set out to reposition the Labour Party on law and order as a means of reconnecting the party with the suburban working class base it had lost to the Conservatives during the Thatcher era. After the shocking murder by two children of toddler Jamie Bulger in February 1993, Blair grabbed the moment, making a notable speech in the town of Wellingborough in Northamptonshire on 19 February. The crimes, he said, were a manifestation of a society that had broken down and was not worthy of its name. They were 'hammer blows struck against the sleeping conscience of the country, urging us to wake up and look unflinchingly at what we see'. As well as recognise the breakdown of community, the political left, he said, needed to recognise and teach the moral idea of right and wrong. The speech made an instant impression, marking out Blair as a future leadership contender. What its argument needed was a stand-out line that could encapsulate it in a way that would be remembered and instantly understood, and, latching on to a phrase first used by then Shadow Chancellor Gordon Brown, he found it in a nice piece of *symploce* that has influenced social democratic parties the world over. (It is also an example of *alliteration*.) It was made in a speech to the annual Labour Party Conference on 30 September 1993.

> Labour is the party of law and order in Britain today. Tough on crime and tough on the causes of crime.

**Tricolon:** *speaking in threes to emphasise points*

The Tory party has always had a problem convincing the British people that their National Health System is safe in their hands – given the party's belief in privatisation. Opposition to the NHS became a painful symbol of the party's failure to move to the centre ground – until the leadership of David Cameron. Dismissed as an Eton-educated toff, Cameron used his address to the Conservative Party conference on 3 October 2006 to convince the electorate that he was an ordinary guy; and what better way to do it than spell out his personal debt to the public medical system. Mimicking Tony Blair's well-known *tricolon* about education (which itself mimicked Demosthenes' description about the three most important aspects of oratory – delivery, delivery, delivery), Cameron's speechwriters produced the delightful threesome at the end of this passage. Note also the *antemetabole*, which reverses 'the NHS is safe in my hands'. Readers will also notice the use of *ethos* and *pathos* – everyone admires the sacrifices of our doctors, nurses and hospital staff and wants to identify with any praise of them. But this passage is even richer in rhetorical technique than that. The audience would have been aware of the reason for Cameron's unstated debt to the NHS: a son born with cerebral palsy and epilepsy, who later died. This made his speech a highly moving example of *praeteritio*.

> When your family relies on the NHS all the time – day after day, night after night – you really know just how precious it is. I know the problems. Turning up at A and E and the children's one is closed. Waiting for the doctor when you're desperate with worry. Waiting for the scan that is so desperately needed. It can be incredibly frustrating. But more often than not, it is an inspiration – thanks to the people who work in the NHS. The nurses who do everything to make you comfortable. The doctors who desperately want to get to the truth. And the army of support staff who get forgotten so often but who make such a difference to all of us.

David Cameron steals Blair's crown under the gaze of the master. Photo: © Getty Images.

For me, it's not a question of saying the NHS is 'safe in my hands'. My family is so often in the hands of the NHS. And I want them to be safe there.

Tony Blair once explained his priority in three words: 'education, education, education. I can do it in three letters: NHS.'

## 4

The figures of speech described above, particularly the schemes, alert us to another element of style: rhythm. As Cicero explains:

If they have similar case endings, or if the clauses are equally balanced, or if contrary ideas are opposed, the sentence becomes rhythmical by its very nature, even if no rhythm is intended.

But rhythm can also be pursued more directly by imitating verse. Rhythm's charms are obvious. By helping words flow, it prevents speakers stumbling through lines and makes it easier for the ear to accept them. Again, while audiences usually have little understanding of the technical aspects of rhythmical language, they know it when they hear it, and they know what they like and what they don't. The Ancients once again came to our aid with a system of classification of rhythm based on the concept of *meter.*

Meter is a system for classifying the regularly occurring patterns of rhythm that occur in prose and verse. While the terminology can be daunting, it is surprisingly simple to grasp.

To determine the meter being used, each individual line of speech is analysed in two ways.

---

**Determining meter**

| Type of stress | Number of feet |
| --- | --- |
| By sorting out which syllables are stressed (⁻) and which unstressed (˘) relative to each other and by determining what recurring pattern they create. This recurring pattern is called a *foot.* While six types of feet are used to classify verse, usually only four are found in speech:<br>• *iambic:* a light followed by a stressed syllable<br>• *anapaestic:* two light syllables followed by a stressed syllable<br>• *trochaic:* a stressed followed by a light syllable<br>• *dactylic:* a stressed syllable followed by two light syllables. | By counting how many instances of these recurring patterns of stress the line contains. There are eight:<br>• *monometer:* one foot<br>• *dimeter:* two feet<br>• *trimeter:* three feet<br>• *tetrameter:* four feet<br>• *pentameter:* five feet<br>• *hexameter:* six feet<br>• *heptameter:* seven feet<br>• *octameter:* eight feet. |

---

Putting these together gives us the type of meter used. For instance, a line containing five repetitions (feet) of a light followed by a stressed syllable is called iambic pentameter; four feet of a stressed followed by a light syllable is called trochaic tetrameter, and so on.

One of the most dramatic speeches in Australian political history provides a fine example. On 11 November 1975, the government of the radical, reforming Labor Prime Minister Gough Whitlam was dismissed by the head of state, the Governor-General Sir John Kerr, in an episode regarded by the left as a conservative constitutional coup, and by the right as a necessary exercise of constitutional reserve powers. Standing on the steps of the parliament building, Whitlam listened calmly as the Governor-General's secretary read out the proclamation of dismissal, and then stepped forward to address the crowd that had gathered spontaneously as rumours of the drama spread. It was a model of defiance, containing the following lines, which can be repeated on cue by every Australian of a certain age.

> Wĕll māy | wĕ sāy | 'Gŏd sāve | thĕ Quēen',
> Bēcaŭse | nōthĭng | wīll savĕ | thē Gŏv|ērnŏr-|Gēnerăl.

The first line is *iambic tetrameter*, the second *trochaic pentameter*.

Gough Whitlam – the noblest Australian of them all. Photo: National Library of Australia, an-24355085

Later that afternoon he made a further address, which is just as widely known. It was blunter, but still managed to be poetic, constituting *iambic bimeter*; utterly repeatable, it became the Labor

Party's de facto campaign slogan and has lived on in the party's folk memory ever since.

Măintāin | yŏur rāge.

# 5

🐾 🐾 🐾

One always expected prose meter from the classically educated Whitlam, who in a previous life would certainly have been a Roman senator. But, delivered off the cuff, the meter of his Dismissal Day speeches is likely unintentional. And this highlights the fact that while antithetic and metric rhythm can be planned, it usually works best when it isn't. Cicero was adamant that rhythm should course naturally; it should not be studied and artificial but flow from thought. Addressing a political rally sounding like a romantic poet or a try-hard Lincoln, risks laughter. The Greeks knew this. The orator Demosthenes was mocked for producing speeches that, while supposedly spontaneous, had the stink of the midnight oil – a long night's hard work.

Politicians and the people close to them quickly learn this, but sometimes they just can't help themselves. From season 2, episode 5 of the television series *The West Wing*, here's the new White House junior counsel, Ainsley Hayes, being reminded by her boss on her first day on the job that she should resist the urge to artificially 'orate when talking to colleagues:

**Ainsley Hayes**: Mr Tribbey? I'd like to do well on this, my first assignment. Any advice you could give me that might point me the way of success would be, by me, appreciated.
**Lionel Tribbey**: Well, not speaking in iambic pentameter might be a step in the right direction.

She wasn't exactly, but the point is taken.

Not everyone does resist, though. Let's look at this construction by speechwriter Michael Gerson, for President George W. Bush's second inaugural address:

America, in this young century, proclaims liberty
throughout all the world, and to all the inhabitants thereof.
Renewed in our strength – tested, but not weary – we are
ready for the greatest achievements in the history of
freedom.

The speech's ambition is plain, to spread freedom, but the use of
*archaism* (outdated words like 'thereof') and *parenthesis* ('tested,
but not weary') are unnecessary affectations. It's as if the speechwriter is saying: 'Hey, it's an inaugural; I can do that Lincoln
thing too!' It can only do the speaker harm. On this occasion it
made Bush – an authentic and often highly effective 'plain blunt'
speaker – look out of his oratorical depth, reminding us of the
old saying that a man never looks shorter than when he's wearing
platform shoes.

George W. Bush – the true 'plain blunt speaker'. Photo: © Jason
Grower/Shutterstock.com.

Tellingly, Bush sounds better when Gerson, who is known for
the religiosity of his speeches, sticks to biblical themes, like 'axis
of evil' or this from later in this same address (which is a far
more natural-sounding example of *iambic hexameter* followed by

*antithesis* and *antanaclasis* (repetition of a word whose meaning changes – 'almighty' and 'all'):

> Frĕedōm | iš nōt | Ămēr| ĭcā's | gīft tō | thĕ wōrld,|
> it's the almighty God's gift to all humanity.

Cicero understood that when it comes to creating rhythm, subtlety is the speaker's watchword. If they suspect they're being manipulated by sensory device, the audience will push back:

> If you use it constantly, it not only wearies the audience, but
> even the layman recognises the nature of the trick:
> furthermore, it takes the feeling out of the delivery, it robs
> the audience of their natural sympathy, and utterly destroys
> the impression of sincerity.

Successful use of figures and rhythm requires judgement about propriety. It needs to be matched to the words and the gravity of the occasion, and not over-done. It should be used sparingly and tellingly to create memorable sound bites. If every line in a speech sang the speaker would be reciting verse not reading prose (as the first great orator Gorgias did – which led Cicero to dismiss his work as mere 'embroidery').

While speakers who employ too many stylistic techniques can be dismissed as feeble, those who employ none 'can possess no force or vigour' – as the stumbling words of boring, inarticulate, bullying politicians prove every day. The speechwriter's ultimate frustration is the last-minute insertion by the chief of staff of 'just a few' qualifying words that break up the carefully balanced flow of words and destroy the intended effect. Instead of smooth rhythm the sound is like the mismatched gears on a truck stripping their teeth. There's certainly nothing effeminate about the lines Peggy Noonan wrote for Ronald Reagan on the fortieth anniversary of D-Day, 6 June 1984, about the US Rangers who took the cliffs above Normandy:

Thĕse arē | thĕ bōys | ŏf Poiñte | dŭ Hōc. | Thĕse arē | thĕ mēn | whŏ tōok | thĕ cliffs.| These are the champions who helped free a continent. These are the heroes who helped end a war.

The first two sentences are *iambic tetrameter*, and the second two have a rhythm that flows from the use of *antithesis* ('boys' to 'men') and the effect of *accumulation* (they 'took the cliffs' . . . 'helped free a continent' . . . and 'helped end a war', no less). One of the finest speeches of the twentieth century, its poetic force was acknowledged by Reagan himself, who compared it to John McCrae's moving First World War poem, *In Flanders Fields*.

> In Flanders fields the poppies blow
> Between the crosses, row on row,
>     That mark our place; and in the sky
> The larks, still bravely singing, fly
>     Scarce heard amid the guns below.
>
> We are the Dead. Short days ago
> We lived, felt dawn, saw sunset glow,
>     Loved, and were loved, and now we lie
>         In Flanders fields.
>
> Take up our quarrel with the foe:
> To you from failing hands we throw
>     The torch; be yours to hold it high.
> If ye break faith with us who die
>     We shall not sleep, though poppies grow
>         In Flanders fields.

## 6

Reagan was right; in the hands of a master speechwriter like Peggy Noonan, great speeches can have the rhythmical and emotional effect of great poetry. Or of great music.

When figurative speech is employed well, what we notice isn't each individual technique but the overall effect. Let's examine more closely Winston Churchill's famous quote in praise of the pilots of RAF Fighter Command, discussed in chapter 3:

Nĕvĕr | iñ thĕ | fiēld ŏf |hūmăn |cōnflĭčt |
was so much owed by so many to so few.

Breaking it down, we grasp how it works and why it's so memorable:

- The first thing you notice is the rhythm. The first clause is *trochaic pentameter*; the rhythm of the second is irregular but is based on repetition.
- It then becomes an *anaphora*, based on the recurrence of 'so'.
- This is in the form of a *tricolon* which reveals itself also as a *parallelism*, each phrase having a similar construction.
- And, listening again, you notice both lines are part of an *isocolon* – having two equal clauses of syllables joined by the conjunction 'was'.
- Then there's *ethos* that gives it its moral force.

The cumulative effect is like listening to a piece of music develop, unfold and pull you in. A classic example is the Paul McCartney song 'Penny Lane', which uses complex harmonies and chord structures to create mood changes for the listener:

- It has a simple cyclical structure of verse – verse – chorus – verse – verse – chorus – verse – verse – chorus – chorus.
- The arrangement is more complicated, complete with brass, flutes, strings and fire bells, creating a sense of nostalgia, suitable for the subject matter of the lyrics.
- The lyrics are sweet, but the verses have an ominous undercurrent that is caused by minor key elements in the harmony

that help create tension and darkness. This prevents the song from being too sickly sweet.

- There is a constant shifting of chord structures and harmonies that draw out emotional responses that relate to the lyrics and help the song move between the major and minor keys.

- The chorus has a higher melody than the verse, and a simple harmony in the major key, giving a feeling of joy and release when it hits. The last chorus really peaks, with a rise in key, leaving the listener in euphoria.

When similarly well composed, speeches work on the intellect, the senses and the emotions in a comparable way. When all these buttons are pushed – especially when delivered by master orators as consumate at speaking as the Beatles were at playing – it becomes the grand style of oratory.

# 7

The high stakes and the huge audiences with their sense of anticipation make US presidential nominating conventions (the bodies that nominate the parties' candidates for president) the perfect occasions for the grand style of oratory that uses the full range of figurative speaking and rhythmical prose. In 2008 both Barack Obama's and Sarah Palin's speechwriting teams proved that they were masters of classical technique. Consciously or unconsciously, they injected these prime-time speeches with many of the same tropes, schemes and rhythms as Brutus, Antony and Cicero would likely have used in the original classical forum of republican Rome. They proved that style isn't just for the sort of display speech that Noonan and Reagan were so adept at writing and delivering; it's for tough political speech as well. If you want to know why Obama's and Palin's speeches stand out from the many thousands made every year, this is why. Here is Obama speaking to the 2008 Democratic National Convention:

**Barack Obama speaking to the 2008 Democratic National Convention**

| | |
|---|---|
| John McCain \| hăs vŏtēd \| wĭth Geŏrge Bŭsh \|nĭñety pĕr cēnt \| ŏf thĕ tīme. Senator McCain likes to talk about judgement, but, really, what does it say about your judgement when you think George Bush has been right more than ninety per cent of the time? [APPLAUSE] | *Anapaestic*: pentameter *epiphora*: repeats 'judgement' and 'ninety per cent of the time' *erotema:* rhetorical question |
| I don't know about you, but I am not ready to take a ten per cent chance on change. [APPLAUSE] | *alliteration*: '10 per cent chance on change' |
| Now, I don't believe that Senator McCain doesn't care what's going on in the lives of Americans; I just think he doesn't know. (LAUGHTER) | *antithesis*: 'doesn't care' versus 'doesn't know' |
| Why else would he define middle class as someone making under $5 million a year? How else could he propose hundreds of billions in tax breaks for big corporations and oil companies, but not one penny of tax relief to more than 100 million Americans? | *praeteritio*: he actually does think McCain doesn't know (and repeats it below in case the audience missed it) |
| How else could he offer a health care plan that would actually tax people's benefits, or an education plan that would do nothing to help families pay for college, or a plan that would privatise Social Security and gamble your retirement? [AUDIENCE BOOS] | *pysma*: multiple rhetorical questions *antithesis*: 'billions' versus 'pennies', 'big business' versus '100 million Americans', 'care' versus 'get' |
| It's not because John McCain doesn't care; it's because John McCain doesn't get it. [APPLAUSE] | *hyperbole*: 'gamble your retirement' |
| For over two decades, he's subscribed to that old, discredited Republican philosophy: give more and more to those with the most and hope that prosperity trickles down to everyone else. | *antanaclasis*: 'own' in 'ownership' changes its meaning *pysma*: multiple rhetorical questions |
| In Washington, they call this the 'Ownership Society', but what it really means is that you're on your own. Out | *epiphora*: repeats 'You're on your own.' *anaphora*: repeats 'it's time' |

*(cont.)*

STYLE

**117**

of work? Tough luck, you're on your own. No health care? The market will fix it. You're on your own. Born into poverty? Pull yourself up by your own bootstraps, even if you don't have boots. You are on your own. [APPLAUSE]

Well, | ĭt's tīme | fŏr thĕm | tŏ own | thĕir fāi | uře. | It's timē | fŏr ūs | tŏ chañge Ămēr | ĭcā. | And that's why I'm running for president of the United States. [APPLAUSE]

*iambic pentameter*

John McCain likes to say that he'll follow bin Laden to the gates of hell, but he won't even follow him to the cave where he lives. [BIG APPLAUSE]

*antithesis*: 'gates of hell' versus 'cave where he lives'

The men and women who serve in our battlefields may be Democrats and Republicans and independents, but they have fought together, and bled together, and some died together under the same proud flag. They have not served a red America or a blue America; they have served the United States of America. [APPLAUSE]

*tricolon*: 'Democrats, Republicans and independents';
*epiphora*: 'fought together', 'bled together', 'died together' (also *tricolon*)
*antithesis*: not served 'red America' or 'blue America' but 'United States of America' (also *tricolon* and *epiphora*)

I get it. I realise that I am not the likeliest candidate for this office. I don't fit the typical pedigree, and I haven't spent my career in the halls of Washington.
But I stand before you tonight because all across America something is stirring. What the naysayers don't understand is that this election has never been about me; it's about you. [APPLAUSE]

*praeteritio*: what he's really saying is that it doesn't matter that he's African-American
*antithesis*: not about 'me' but about 'you'

THE ART OF GREAT SPEECHES

**118**

**Barack Obama speaking to the 2008 Democratic National Convention (*cont.*)**

| | |
|---|---|
| America, we cannot turn back ... [APPLAUSE] ... not with so much work to be done; not with so many children to educate, and so many veterans to care for; not with an economy to fix, and cities to rebuild, and farms to save; not with so many families to protect and so many lives to mend. America, we cannot turn back. We cannot walk alone. At this moment, in this election, we must pledge once more to march into the future. Let us keep that promise, that American promise, and in the words of scripture hold firmly, without wavering, to the hope that we confess. | *climax*: he accelerates to the conclusion<br>*anaphora*: 'not with' and 'so many' and 'we cannot' repeated<br>*polysyndeton*: 'and', 'and'<br>*epiphora*: 'promise' repeated<br><br>*praeteritio*: assumes the audience knows this famous quote from Martin Luther King |

Obama used style here to present himself as the dignified grand orator, playing to the strengths that won him the primary campaign. Sarah Palin in her Republican National Convention speech, by contrast, was folksier. But while her rhetoric may have been contrived to sound unaffected, as we can see from the following excerpts, it was just as rich in classical technique.

**Sarah Palin's speech to the 2008 Republican Convention**

| | |
|---|---|
| With their usual certitude, they [the experts in Washington] told us that all was lost, there was no hope for this candidate [John McCain], who said that he would rather lose an election than see his country lose a war. But the pollsters... [APPLAUSE] the pollsters and the pundits, they overlooked just one thing when they wrote him off. They overlooked the calibre of the man himself, the determination, and resolve, and the sheer guts of Senator John McCain. [APPLAUSE] | *antithesis*: 'he' versus 'his country' and 'lose an election' versus 'lose a war'<br><br>*alliteration*: 'pollsters and pundits'<br>*polysyndeton*: 'and' |

STYLE

(*cont.*)    **119**

**Sarah Palin's speech to the 2008 Republican Convention (*cont.*)**

| | |
|---|---|
| The voters knew better, and maybe that's because they realised there's a time for politics and a time for leadership, a time to campaign and a time to put our country first. [APPLAUSE] | *anaphora*: repetition of 'a time' <br> *antithesis*: 'politics' versus 'leadership' and 'campaign' versus 'patriotism' <br> *parallelism*: ends with repetition of two main and two subordinate clauses |
| Here's a little newsflash for those reporters and commentators: I'm not going to Washington to seek their good opinion. I'm going to Washington to serve the people of this great country. [APPLAUSE] | *anaphora*: 'I'm' and 'going' <br><br> *antithesis*: 'their good opinion' versus 'the people of this great country' |
| Americans expect us to go to Washington for the right reason and not just to mingle with the right people. Politics isn't just a game of clashing parties and competing interests. The right reason is to challenge the status quo, to serve the common good, and to leave this nation better than we found it. [APPLAUSE] | *antanaclasis*: repetition of 'right' but the meaning changes from pejorative to positive (making it an *antithesis*) <br> *alliteration*: 'clashing parties and competing interests'; 'clear convictions' <br> *anaphora*: repetition of 'right reason' |
| No one expects us all to agree on everything, but we are expected to govern with integrity, and goodwill, and clear convictions, and a servant's heart. | |
| And I pledge to all Americans that I will carry myself in this spirit as vice president of the United States. | *tricolon*: 'challenge ...', 'serve ...' and 'leave ...' <br> *polysyndeton*: repetition of 'and' |
| We need American sources of resources. We need American energy brought to you by American ingenuity and produced by American workers. [APPLAUSE] | *paronomasia*: similarity of 'sources' and 'resources' <br> *epiphora*: repetition of 'American' |
| America needs more energy; our opponent is against producing it. Victory in Iraq is finally in sight, | *accumulation*: forceful summary of preceding arguments |

| | |
|---|---|
| and he wants to forfeit. Terrorist states are seeking nuclear weapons without delay; he wants to meet them without preconditions. | *hyperbole*: exaggerating her opponent's intentions and weaknesses |
| Al Qaida terrorists still plot to inflict catastrophic harm on America, and he's worried that someone won't read them their rights. [APPLAUSE] | *sarcasm*: read terrorists their rights? |
| Government is too big; he wants to grow it. Congress spends too much money; he promises more. Taxes are too high, and he wants to raise them. His tax increases are the fine print in his economic plan. | *epiphora* and *antithesis*: 'without delay' versus 'without preconditions'; 'inflict harm' versus 'read them their rights' |
| And let me be specific: The Democratic nominee for president supports plans to raise income taxes, and raise payroll taxes, and raise investment income taxes, and raise the death tax, and raise business taxes, and increase the tax burden on the American people by hundreds of billions of dollars. | *parallelism*, *tricolon*, *anaphora*: three similarly structured sentences ('...; he ...') |
| | *alliteration*: 'fine print' and 'economic plan' |
| | *anaphora*: repetition of 'raise' |
| | *polysyndeton*: repetition of 'and' |
| | *accumulation*: speedier repetition of the ideas above |

Palin's masterpiece in this speech is to project subtly the common touch of the outsider while employing the rhetorical sophistication of the insiders she's denouncing. The parallel with Mark Antony in his speech following Brutus is obvious. And the similarity is even more apparent as she uses her most devastating lines in the speech to accuse Barack Obama of being silver-tongued. Ironically, like Antony's claim that he has

neither wit, nor words, nor worth,
Action, nor utterance, nor the power of speech
to stir men's blood,

it is one of the most technically sophisticated passages of her address. And, as the game-shooting, proudly provincial Palin admits in her memoir, it wasn't written by a plain blunt speaker, but by her sophisticated, professional speechwriter – George W. Bush's former speechwriter Matthew Scully – 'a bunny-hugging vegan' and member of the cultural elite, no less, whom, she informs us, 'was very generous about letting me add my own words'. Here it is.

---

**Sarah Palin's speech to the 2008 Republican Convention (*cont.*)**

---

And now, I've noticed a pattern with our opponent, and maybe you have, too. We've all heard his dramatic speeches before devoted followers, and there is much to like and admire about our opponent.

*antonomasia*: she's crediting the audience with perceptiveness

*sarcasm*: she is mocking his achievements

But listening to him speak, it's easy to forget that this is a man who has authored two memoirs but not a single major law or even a reform, not even in the State Senate. [APPLAUSE]

*antithesis*: 'two memoirs' versus 'single major law'

*sarcasm*: mocking his priorities

This is a man who can give an entire speech about the wars America is fighting and never use the word 'victory', except when he's talking about his own campaign. [APPLAUSE]

*anaphora*: repetition of 'when the'

*sarcasm*: mocking his pretentiousness

But when the cloud of rhetoric has passed, when the roar of the crowd fades away, when the stadium lights go out, and those styrofoam Greek columns are hauled back to some studio lot...[APPLAUSE] when that happens, what exactly is our opponent's plan? What does he actually seek to accomplish after he's done turning back the waters and healing the planet? [APPLAUSE]

*anthypophora*: she asks and then answers her own rhetorical questions

The answer – the answer is to make government bigger, and take more of your money, and give you more orders from Washington, and to reduce the strength of America in a dangerous world.

*polysyndeton*: repetition of 'and'

THE ART OF GREAT SPEECHES

# 8

ᕟ ᕟ ᕟ

It is interesting to note the change in shade of the analysis in the right-hand column compared to that between Brutus and Antony. On this occasion it's the political right that has played stylishly, and the left that has played the more brutal game of using rhetoric to re-interpret its opponent's meaning and intentions. Cicero, we suspect, would have approved. As we saw in Shakespeare's version of the debate over Caesar's butchered body, Brutus' command of rhetorical style was turned against him by the equally sophisticated but more subtle, crafty and ruthless Antony. In real life, Cicero pre-warned Brutus of the dangers of formality and aristocratic reserve and of the need for defenders of the Republic to do whatever was necessary to win over the masses.

In the chapters that follow, we will see how Cicero and his classical contemporaries believed this should be done – and whether the liberal Barack Obama was fully awake to the challenge. As we shall see, employing schemes and tropes is the easy part.

# Chapter 5
# Emotion

## 1

It's difficult to make political consultants cry. As experts in the art of manipulation, they've seen every move. So if you can bring *them* to tears, you've done something extraordinary.

In their account of the 2008 US presidential election, the journalists John Heilemann and Mark Halperin relate just such an extraordinary event involving Barack Obama's address to the Democratic National Convention. In his peroration, Obama alluded (using the technique of *praeteritio* discussed in the previous chapter) to the fact that he was speaking on the 45th anniversary of the Reverend Martin Luther King's 'I have a dream' speech on the Washington Mall in 1963 (the use of 'but' in *epiphora* in the first paragraph was a signature technique of Dr King, as Obama's speechwriting team would have known):

> This country of ours has more wealth than any nation,
> but that's not what makes us rich. We have the most
> powerful military on Earth, but that's not what makes us
> strong. Our universities and our culture are the envy of the

world, but that's not what keeps the world coming to our shores.

Instead, it is that American spirit, that American promise, that pushes us forward even when the path is uncertain; that binds us together in spite of our differences; that makes us fix our eye not on what is seen, but what is unseen, that better place around the bend.

That promise is our greatest inheritance. It's a promise I make to my daughters when I tuck them in at night and a promise that you make to yours, a promise that has led immigrants to cross oceans and pioneers to travel west, a promise that led workers to picket lines and women to reach for the ballot. [APPLAUSE]

And it is that promise that, 45 years ago today, brought Americans from every corner of this land to stand together on a mall in Washington, before Lincoln's Memorial, and hear a young preacher from Georgia speak of his dream. [APPLAUSE]

The men and women who gathered there could've heard many things. They could've heard words of anger and discord. They could've been told to succumb to the fear and frustrations of so many dreams deferred.

But what the people heard instead – people of every creed and colour, from every walk of life – is that, in America, our destiny is inextricably linked, that together our dreams can be one.

'We cannot walk alone,' the preacher cried. 'And as we walk, we must make the pledge that we shall always march ahead. We cannot turn back.'

America, we cannot turn back . . .

At this point, the reporters tell us, Obama's two tough-minded chief advisers David Axelrod and Robert Gibbs were in tears, as were many in the audience. This is even more remarkable for the fact that they would have been familiar with the words, having read and re-read countless drafts and watched the candidate's autocue rehearsals in the days and weeks preceding – even mouthing the words along with the speaker, anxiously hoping he didn't blow it like Neil Armstrong. (This is what modern speechwriters do during the big launch, as they sit next to the autocue operator.)

But the Democratic candidate's soaring rhetoric provoked a different emotional response from his opponents – not joyful tears but anger – as shown by the reaction of the Republican Convention's delegates to the derisive assessment of Obama's oratory and character offered by Sarah Palin near the end of chapter 4.

Two audiences, two contrasting reactions. Palin was exploiting the fact that a Democrat's appeals were bound to provoke opposite emotional reactions from Republicans. Immune to the emotional pull of the civil rights movement, labour unions and the liberal idea of 'progress', conservatives were left asking, 'where's the substance and why should we take such unworldly optimism seriously?' It's a political game that will be played over and over again, one expects, until the end of politics itself.

# 2

What those differing reactions illustrate is something that Aristotle, Cicero and other classical thinkers understood well: logic and facts are only part of the orator's arsenal, often the least devastating, and the effect of a speech depends to a major degree on the state of mind and the standpoint of the audience. As Aristotle observed in the courts and assemblies of his day, the same logic and facts

do not seem the same to those who love and those who
hate, not to those who are angry and those who are calm,
but either altogether different and different in magnitude.
For to the friend the man about whom he is giving
judgement seems either to have committed no offence or a

minor one, while for the enemy it is the opposite. And to the man who is enthusiastic and optimistic, if what is to come should be pleasant, it seems to be both likely to come about and likely to be good, while to the indifferent and depressed man it seems the opposite.

In other words, the orator's task isn't just to present a watertight case but to understand the psychology of the audience and use that understanding to try to breach its emotional as well as logical defences. To Aristotle, tapping emotions wasn't an add-on or a trick but one of the orator's main tasks – because he believed that the proof of a case was provided not only by the speaker but also by those listening. As any good public speaker knows, even without having read the classical authorities, eliciting the right emotional response from the audience can multiply the force of the logical and factual arguments being made.

This observation is bound to upset logicians and trial judges, who would prefer cases were decided by logic and facts only. The noble-minded appeals to the jury of Hollywood court dramas aside, modern judicial systems are organised specifically to exclude any deviation from the rational presentation of the facts. In a real court you will listen in vain for the emotional summing up of an Atticus Finch:

> There is one way in this country in which all men are created equal – there is one institution that makes a pauper the equal of a Rockefeller, the stupid man the equal of an Einstein and the ignorant man the equal of any college president. That institution, gentlemen, is a court. It can be the Supreme Court of the United States or the humblest J.P. court in the land, or this honourable court which you serve. Our courts have their faults, as does any human institution, but in this country our courts are the great levellers, and in our courts all men are created equal.
>
> I'm no idealist to believe firmly in the integrity our courts, and in the jury system – that is no ideal to me, it is a living,

working reality. Gentlemen, a court is no better than each man of you sitting before me on this jury. A court is only as sound as its jury, and a jury is only as sound as the men who make it up. I am confident that you gentlemen will review without passion the evidence you have heard, come to a decision, and restore this defendant to his family. In the name of God, do your duty.

Gregory Peck as Atticus Finch – proving that courtroom speeches are usually better in fiction. Photo: © Getty Images.

A trial lawyer is more likely to spend hours of well-paid time casting doubt on forensic procedure or musing over the size of a glove than soliloquising about the nature of justice. Outside the courts, though, just as in Athens and Rome, anything still goes. The political speaker isn't judged by a panel of scientifically objective philosophers or Supreme Court justices but by voters. Cicero knew that:

the real quality of an orator can only be deduced from the *practical results* his speech making obtains.

The goal is to win, and winning requires three things: instructing listeners, gaining their sympathy and vigorously moving their emotions. The first, the use of logic and facts, is the subject of chapter 7. The second, a form of emotional appeal based on the believability of the speaker, is discussed in chapter 6. But the third, moving the emotions, is potentially the most effective appeal, mastered only by the greatest practitioners, and it's easy to tell when they're doing it successfully:

> When someone is listening to an authentic orator, he believes what he hears, he is sure that it is true, he agrees and applauds: the orator has convinced him ... The listening multitude is delighted, finds itself carried along by what he says, is pervaded by a sort of pleasurable excitement. There is nothing you can take exception to in that. They feel joyful, they feel sorrowful, they laugh, they cry, they are moved to show sympathy or hatred, contempt, envy, pity, shame, disgust. They are angry, or amazed, or hopeful, or terrified. And all of this happens because the minds and hearts of these listeners are worked up by the words and sentiments and delivery of the orator.

Aristotle lists ten emotions that good orators can exploit; four of them positive and six negative, although we could add many more.

---

**Emotions that a good orator can exploit**

| Positive emotions | Negative emotions |
| --- | --- |
| calm | anger |
| friendship | fear |
| favour | shame |
| pity | indignation |
| | envy |
| | jealousy |

---

Cicero further observes that emotion works best when it is used in the *exordium* (opening) where it prepares the audience for what is to come, and in the *peroration* (conclusion) where it follows the summing up of the case by inciting ill will against an opponent's case and generating sympathy for the speaker's case. Emotion closes the deal made possible by logic, facts and the speaker's credibility and delivery.

All of us are occasionally moved by the emotional appeals of speechmakers. How do they do it? How do they penetrate our logical defences without us realising, or, when we do realise, with our complicity? There are four major techniques: simile and metaphor, storytelling, amplification and the presentation of emotional topics.

# 3

First, let's look at simile and metaphor.

David Puttnam and Hugh Hudson's 1981 Academy Award winning *Chariots of Fire* is widely regarded as one of the great British films. It's not hard to see why. It's sumptuously filmed, has an appealing and heroic story arc full of memorable scenes, a cast of actors so perfect for their roles that their careers were largely defined by them, a great soundtrack, and a hugely popular theme, the Olympic Games. But people love it because it's not really about sport at all. It's a metaphor for something every moviegoer has to face: how to remain good as we compete to achieve our ambitions. The races – the Trinity College courtyard dash, Harold Abrahams' 100 metres and Eric Liddell's 400 metres – are metaphors for life itself. It comes as no surprise therefore that one of the film's most memorable scenes is a speech made by the Scottish Liddell after the Scotland versus Ireland races, which uses the running of a race as a simile for maintaining religious faith. Where, he asks, as the sunshine breaks through the rain clouds, does the power to win life's race come from? 'From within.' The actor playing Liddell, Ian Charleson, who tragically died of AIDS in 1990 at the age of just 40, was able to deliver it with such understated passion partly because he wrote it himself. Having got the role of the devout runner, who later became a renowned Presbyterian missionary in China,

Charleson studied the Bible to get inside his character (reputedly turning up to the audition carrying a copy of the good book and proclaiming 'I've read half of it – I think it's rather good') and decided that the original script was far too high tone for the circumstances of its delivery to a working class audience huddled under umbrellas in the pouring rain on a racing track. The result, if you watch the film, is a speech that not only meets Cicero's demand for propriety but is also quietly moving.

Liddell's speech contrasts sharply with another emotive, metaphorical speech consistently voted the greatest and most memorable of all time: Martin Luther King's famous 'I have a dream' speech to 200 000 expectant people on the Washington Mall and tens of millions more on television on 23 August 1963. Ironically, while a written text, loaded with grand oratorical style, the speech is remembered mostly for its stirring peroration, which was made off the cuff after the soul singer Mahalia Jackson, close to the podium, yelled out to King to divert from his text and tell them about his dream. She was referring to a metaphor King had employed before, most recently during a big speech in Detroit, where he used a dream to describe a possible future in which the United States lived out the principles of the *Declaration of Independence* and all races lived in equality and harmony. As the passage below demonstrates, King's southern Baptist preacher style relies on the traditional techniques of the classical orator – *anaphora, asyndeton, antithesis, parallelism* and *prose rhythm (iambic dimeter* – I hăvē | ă drēam) – the poetic effect of which combine with the metaphor to give it added emotional force:

Even though we face the difficulties of today and tomorrow, I still have a dream. It is a dream deeply rooted in the American dream.

I have a dream that one day this nation will rise up and live out the true meaning of its creed: 'We hold these truths to be self-evident, that all men are created equal'.

I have a dream that one day on the red hills of Georgia, the sons of former slaves and the sons of former slave owners will be able to sit down together at the table of brotherhood.

I have a dream that one day even the state of Mississippi, a state sweltering with the heat of injustice, sweltering with the heat of oppression, will be transformed into an oasis of freedom and justice.

I have a dream that my four little children will one day live in a nation where they will not be judged by the colour of their skin but by the content of their character.

I have a dream today!

I have a dream that one day, down in Alabama, with its vicious racists, with its governor having his lips dripping with the words of 'interposition' and 'nullification' – one day right there in Alabama little black boys and black girls will be able to join hands with little white boys and white girls as sisters and brothers.

I have a dream today!

I have a dream that one day every valley shall be exalted, and every hill and mountain shall be made low, the rough places will be made plain, and the crooked places will be made straight; and the glory of the Lord shall be revealed and all flesh shall see it together.

This is our hope, and this is the faith that I go back to the South with.

With this faith, we will be able to hew out of the mountain of despair a stone of hope. With this faith, we will be able to transform the jangling discords of our nation into a beautiful symphony of brotherhood. With this faith, we will be able to work together, to pray together, to struggle together, to go to jail together, to stand up for freedom together, knowing that we will be free one day.

Martin Luther King makes the world's favourite speech off the cuff on the steps of the Lincoln Memorial. Photo: © AFP/Getty Images.

Liddell's and King's metaphorical speeches are about faith and hope. The Reverend King is associated with another cause of metaphorical *pathos*: tragedy – the idea that he may not live long enough to see the Promised Land envisioned in his famous dream.

On 29 March 1968 King flew to Memphis, Tennessee, to show his support for black sanitation workers striking against employment discrimination. His flight was delayed by a bomb threat, a sign of the constant danger of assassination that now stalked him. On 3 April, at the last-minute plea of his friend Ralph Abernathy, King agreed to address a gathering at the Mason Temple Church. On a humid night, in the middle of a major storm, with lightening illuminating the hall and peals of thunder interrupting his words, King reached into his rhetorical toolbox to speak *extempore* about the dangers he – and by implication America and its civil rights movement – were in, remarking that the dangers were as nothing because he had been to the mountaintop and he had seen the Promised Land. The next day a lone gunman penetrated the protective police cordon around King and shot him dead on the balcony of the Lorraine Hotel where he was staying, ensuring this speech, like 'I have a dream', would live on.

Powerful on the page, like all King's speeches this one is even more commanding on film where King's timing and feel for the audience's response can be fully appreciated. King's speech has the added *pathos* of personal human loss; like any of us he wants to live but knows he's trapped, and his audience knows that there's nobody who more deserves to be there at the end and find out what it's all been for. It's little wonder that by the end of the speech King all but collapsed into the arms of the other preachers waiting beside the podium and that many in the audience were crying:

I got into Memphis. And some began to ... talk about the threats that were out. What would happen to me from some of our sick white brothers?

Well, I don't know what will happen now. We've got some difficult days ahead. But it really doesn't matter with me now, because I've been to the mountaintop. [AUDIENCE: 'YEAH', APPLAUSE]

And I don't mind.

Like anybody, I would like to live a long life. Longevity has its place. But I'm not concerned about that now. I just want to do God's will. ['YEAH'] And He's allowed me to go up to the mountain. ['YEAH'] And I've looked over. ['YEAH'] And I've seen the Promised Land. [CHEERS] I may not get there with you. But I want you to know tonight, that we, as a people, will get to the Promised Land! [CHEERS, APPLAUSE]

And so I'm happy, tonight.

I'm not worried about anything.

I'm not fearing any man!

Mine eyes have seen the glory of the coming of the Lord! [APPLAUSE]

Having read or watched this, it's easy to understand the power of Barack Obama's convention-night invocation of King – the personification of liberal tragedy – and its effect on his minders. Just mentioning him invokes hope and tragedy. Steeped in American liberal politics, they understood that their candidate – the inheritor of King's leadership and oratorical genius – is going to be the one to make it down the mountain to the rich valley below.

The mountaintop, the journey, the race, dreams, self-awakenings, walls crashing down – these are common and, in the hands of a King, powerful religious metaphors which lend themselves easily to art and oratory. But you don't have to be a King to use them. One of the most famous Australian speeches, by postwar Labor leader Ben Chifley, was based around 'the light on the hill'. With the right sort of speaker and audience at your disposal, a competent speechwriter can employ metaphors like these with confidence. Let me give you an example.

During the 2007 federal election campaign in Australia, the Labor leader, Kevin Rudd, frequently described the difficulty of winning back office after eleven years in opposition as a steep and difficult climb from the base camp of Mount Everest. Strangely, he made no use of this obvious and dramatic metaphor after his victory. (I actually drafted some passages around this metaphor for his election night speech, but, remembering the speechwriter's moral code – see chapter 10, section 6 – resisted the urge to send them through.) Pondering what to write for the darling of Labor's rank and file, Julia Gillard, for the party's first national conference after claiming government, the Everest metaphor came back to me, with its emotive potential to evoke a quest, sacrifice, loss and redemption. The metaphor also provided something else such a speech needed: a vantage point from which a possible future could be surveyed. In an otherwise rhetorically lacklustre conference it stole the applause and the headlines. Given the audience – hundreds of true believers begging to be uplifted – it was hard to believe that no one else, Rudd especially, had recognised the opportunity his metaphor represented. It was a failure that illustrated dramatically

Rudd's unwillingness to inspire through speech or trust the talents of his speechwriters. And it ceded his party's most important forum to the person who, eleven months later, would replace him as prime minister. Her speech concluded:

> I end by asking you to remember that hard decade in opposition. How tough it was to climb the summit to government. And how good it feels to finally be on top.
>
> Kevin Rudd helped us get there. But staying there is the responsibility of every single one of us in this hall. And of every party member across the country.
>
> So let's commit ourselves over the course of the next three days, and then over the months and years that follow . . . to keep up our work rate . . . keep our minds on the big to picture . . . remain true to our beliefs . . . never be adverse to risk . . . and always maintain our ethical beliefs and reforming impulse.
>
> If we do these things, delegates, we will stay at the top of the mountain and be able to achieve all the great possibilities we can now see stretched out before us.

This is an example of a rule speechwriters should always employ: think of the emotional potentialities of the speech you have to write. Find someone sympathetic who will suffer if the policy you are proposing is or isn't adopted (and by choosing not a helpless victim but someone who can fight back, you will also be able to tap *ethos*). If you're arguing for an increase in the minimum wage, talk about the people who put their lives on the line for little reward, invite them to the speech and ask them to stand up. If it's an economic speech given in a city of extremes – like São Paulo in Brazil – talk about what your proposal will do for the people in the slums. It involves thinking yourself into the situation of the speech and exploiting it to the full.

# 4

At the moment he was shot at the Lorraine Hotel, Martin Luther King had been leaning over the balcony talking to members of his entourage – among them the man who was to inherit his mantle as the supreme American orator, the Reverend Jesse Jackson. Electorally, the times weren't with Jackson, who unsuccessfully contested the Democratic nomination a number of times, but he could hold an audience like few others, and in terms of pure oratory if not political impact, his speeches were the highlights of his party's nominating conventions from the Reagan era to the emergence of Barack Obama. Like most grand orators, Jackson's strength was his use of *pathos*. As Cicero was aware, *pathos* is the most difficult of all qualities to present, and there's no more fraught way of presenting it than through storytelling – the second powerful way of appealing to emotion. Only the best can get away with *parable*. And here's Jackson at his best, on 15 August 1992, relating a truly remarkable tale to the Democratic National Convention at a packed Madison Square Garden:

> Not very long ago I was in South Carolina speaking to a small school. I saw a strange and unusual sight. I saw a six-feet-eight athlete walking across the campus holding the hand of a three-foot dwarf. There was this contrast.
>
> It looked to be romantic. She was looking up and he was looking down. They got to the sidewalk, crossed, and she jumped up on the bench and they embraced and kissed. And he gave her her books and she went skipping down the sidewalk.
>
> I tried to act normal, but, Andy, it looked funny to me. [LAUGHTER] I said, 'Mr President, what am I looking at?'
>
> He said: 'Well, I thought you would ask. You see, that is his sister. Matter of fact, it is his twin sister. And by some freak of nature, he came out giant and she came out dwarf. He's a

top athlete in this State. We couldn't afford to get him. All the big schools offered him scholarships. The pros offered him a contract. But he said "I can only go to the college where my sister can get a scholarship." But then they rightly said: "We can't give two scholarships. We have bright lights; we have 'pro' possibilities." He said: "But if my sister can't go, I can't go."'

Somewhere that boy learned something about ethics, about real caring, about real character. 'If my sister can't go, I can't go.' [APPLAUSE BREAKING OUT] All of us are not born giants, with silver spoons in our mouths, and gold slippers on our feet. Some of us are born short – short of hope, short of opportunity, abandoned, neglected, homeless, motherless, teeth crooked, eyes tangled, dreams busted, *hurt*!

But somebody has to measure their giant-ness not by leaping up but by reaching back and reaching out and loving and caring and sharing. Democrats, if we pursue that ethic, that love ethic, that care ethic [CHEERS AND APPLAUSE] we will win and deserve to win. Stand tall, never surrender, keep hope alive, keep hope alive, keep hope alive, keep ... hope ... alive. [AUDIENCE JOINS IN THE CHANT]

With its *pathos* (and *antithesis*) of giant-ness and dwarfism, romantic and filial love, drive and struggle, small Southern colleges and the Ivy League, ethics and money, Jackson presents a *parable* about the values he wants his party to fight for – and which the audience knows in its heart it should fight for but perhaps won't, or at least not with the fierceness it should. (As we shall see in the following chapter his mention of the giant's character alerts us to the power of another specialised form of appeal – *ethos*.) If you watch the television footage of the speech, you will notice that the panning cameras reveal members of the audience change from expectancy, to bemusement, amusement, amazement and tears.

(It's the old story: Make 'em laugh, make 'em cry.) Even though they expected nothing less than this sort of outrageous rhetorical ploy from Jackson, their almost total emotional surrender illustrated his right to be regarded as an example of one of Cicero's ideal orators.

Jesse Jackson passes Martin Luther King's flame to Barack Obama. Photo: © Getty Images.

Jesse Jackson's amazing story moves by evoking love, hope and sacrifice. At the 2008 Republican Convention Sarah Palin brought her speech to its conclusion with another story – about heroism.

Cool logic suggests that the ability to withstand torture or a fierce artillery bombardment tells us little about a person's beliefs or capacity to conduct the complex business of modern government. (After all, his First World War record suggests Adolf Hitler was nothing if not brave under fire.) But such trials can highlight a certain strength of character and evoke the respect most have for veterans. Palin's speechwriter here zeroes in on the defining moment of her presidential running mate John McCain's life to highlight the strongest element of his political appeal – his war record and commitment to duty. Palin admits she was so moved by the story that rehearsals were halted because it made it her cry. So, during the actual delivery she resolved to 'to just pinch myself and grit my teeth when I came to that part'.

> There is only one man in this election who has ever really fought for you in places where winning means survival and defeat means death. And that man is John McCain. [APPLAUSE] . . .

> [His] is the journey of an upright and honourable man, the kind of fellow whose name you will find on war memorials in small towns across this great country, only he was among those who came home.

> To the most powerful office on Earth, he would bring the compassion that comes from having once been powerless, the wisdom that comes even to the captives by the grace of God, the special confidence of those who have seen evil and have seen how evil is overcome. A fellow . . . [APPLAUSE] a fellow prisoner of war, a man named Tom Moe of Lancaster, Ohio . . . [APPLAUSE] Tom Moe recalls looking through a pinhole in his cell door as Lieutenant Commander John McCain was led down the hallway by the guards, day after day.

> And the story is told, when McCain shuffled back from torturous interrogations, he would turn towards Moe's door, and he'd flash a grin and a thumbs up, as if to say, 'We're going to pull through this.'

> My fellow Americans, that is the kind of man America needs to see us through the next four years. [APPLAUSE]

Sarah Palin's rhetoric puts a true war hero in the shade. Photo: © Christopher Halloran/Shutterstock.com.

For a season, a gifted speaker can inspire with his words. But for a lifetime, John McCain has inspired with his deeds. [APPLAUSE]

Virtually the whole world was watching when the man who eclipsed Jackson and defeated Palin and McCain's candidacy used the peroration of his election night speech to tell a story too. Obama's story was the story of a nation and a century, but he gave it added emotional power by making it the biography of a 106-year-old black woman. In this way it becomes not about history but an appeal to the emotional respect all cultures have to the very elderly. Obama's story isn't just the peroration of his speech; it's the peroration of his campaign. It's also in a very real sense the peroration of the African-American struggle for political equality. The unmentioned person here is the man it's really about – Obama himself – which makes this a form of *praeteritio*. (And the attentive reader of the preceding chapter will observe that it is loaded with many other figurative devices.)

This election had many firsts and many stories that will be told for generations. But one that's on my mind tonight is about a woman who cast her ballot in Atlanta. She's a lot like the millions of others who stood in line to make their voice heard in this election except for one thing – Ann Nixon Cooper is 106 years old.

She was born just a generation past slavery; a time when there were no cars on the road or planes in the sky; when someone like her couldn't vote for two reasons – because she was a woman and because of the colour of her skin.

And tonight, I think about all that she's seen throughout her century in America – the heartache and the hope; the struggle and the progress; the times we were told that we can't, and the people who pressed on with that American creed: Yes we can. [AUDIENCE CHANTS 'YES WE CAN']

At a time when women's voices were silenced and their hopes dismissed, she lived to see them stand up and speak out and reach for the ballot. Yes we can. [CHANT]

When there was despair in the dust bowl and Depression across the land, she saw a nation conquer fear itself with a New Deal, new jobs and a new sense of common purpose. Yes we can. [CHANT]

When the bombs fell on our harbour and tyranny threatened the world, she was there to witness a generation rise to greatness and a democracy was saved. Yes we can. [CHANT]

She was there for the buses in Montgomery, the hoses in Birmingham, a bridge in Selma, and a preacher from Atlanta who told a people that 'We Shall Overcome'. Yes we can. [CHANT]

A man touched down on the moon, a wall came down in Berlin, a world was connected by our own science and imagination. And this year, in this election, she touched her finger to a screen, and cast her vote, because after 106 years in America, through the best of times and the darkest of hours, she knows how America can change. Yes we can. [CHANT]

America, we have come so far. We have seen so much. But there is so much more to do. So tonight, let us ask ourselves – if our children should live to see the next century; if my daughters should be so lucky to live as long as Ann Nixon Cooper, what change will they see? What progress will we have made?

This is our chance to answer that call. This is our moment. This is our time.

# 5

────────────────────  🐾 🐾 🐾  ────────────────────

If you want to move an audience, a third technique is to exaggerate. This is essentially what's meant by the term 'amplification'. Make the threat seem more imminent, the situation more dire, the consequences more disastrous, the loyalty more intense, the betrayal more treacherous. *If you have tears, prepare to shed them now – because we intend to muddle through and make incremental gains* may accurately describe what most politicians really do, but it won't get an audience on its feet, never mind make them cry.

Shakespeare knew this, and, having read his Plutarch and Appian, suspected Mark Antony must have too. This makes Antony's speech a model of the use of amplification to rouse an audience.

Shakespeare's Antony wants his audience to listen with their hearts not just their minds by considering their love of Caesar not the reasoned arguments of Brutus about their recovered liberty – even though he disguises it by the use of *irony*:

> You all did love him [Caesar] once, not without cause:
> What cause withholds you then, to mourn for him?

O judgment! thou art fled to brutish beasts,
And men have lost their reason. Bear with me;
My heart is in the coffin there with Caesar,
And I must pause till it come back to me . . .
if I were disposed to stir
Your hearts and minds to mutiny and rage,
I should do Brutus wrong, and Cassius wrong.

Giving meaning to the cliché about waving a red rag in front of a
bull, Antony draws the audience around Caesar's blood-soaked toga
and shows them the horror of the assassination, providing details
about each dagger thrust that he couldn't possibly have known,
exaggerating (as Brutus himself did for opposite reasons) Caesar's
love for Brutus and therefore the magnitude of his treachery and
ingratitude. The first line here signals Brutus' outrageous pitch for
the plebs' emotions:

If you have tears, prepare to shed them now.
You all do know this mantle: I remember
The first time ever Caesar put it on;
'Twas on a summer's evening, in his tent,
That day he overcame the Nervii:
Look, in this place ran Cassius' dagger through:
See what a rent the envious Casca made:
Through this the well-beloved Brutus stabb'd;
And as he pluck'd his cursed steel away,
Mark how the blood of Caesar follow'd it,
As rushing out of doors, to be resolved
If Brutus so unkindly knock'd, or no;
For Brutus, as you know, was Caesar's angel:
Judge, O you gods, how dearly Caesar loved him!
This was the most unkindest cut of all;
For when the noble Caesar saw him stab,
Ingratitude, more strong than traitors' arms,
Quite vanquish'd him: then burst his mighty heart;

And, in his mantle muffling up his face,
Even at the base of Pompey's statua,
Which all the while ran blood, great Caesar fell.
O, what a fall was there, my countrymen!
Then I, and you, and all of us fell down,
Whilst bloody treason flourish'd over us.
O, now you weep; and, I perceive, you feel
The dint of pity: these are gracious drops.
Kind souls, what, weep you when you but behold
Our Caesar's vesture wounded? Look you here,
Here is himself, marr'd, as you see, with traitors.

By the end of this passage the citizens of Rome share many of the emotions Aristotle had outlined as important: anger, shame, fear, indignation, friendship, favour and pity.


# 6

Shakespeare knew, however, that while words may make people cry, it often takes something additional to make them act – self-interest.

It's for this reason that Antony's speech adopts a further rhetorical trick to heighten the receptive state of the audience: presenting the topic in a way that will appeal to powerful emotions. In this case it is greed. Antony dangles before the crowd the prospect that Caesar has left them riches in his will, which the assassins would deny them. Obviously, being a somewhat ignoble emotion, Antony dresses it up as another, more positive emotion, injustice (making this an example of rhetorical redescription or *paradiastole*):

ANTONY:     But here's a parchment with the seal
            of Caesar;
            I found it in his closet, 'tis his will:
            Let but the commons hear this
            testament –

|                    | Which, pardon me, I do not mean to read – |
|--------------------|---------------------------------------------|

Which, pardon me, I do not mean to
read –
And they would go and kiss dead
Caesar's wounds
And dip their napkins in his sacred
blood,
Yea, beg a hair of him for memory,
And, dying, mention it within their
wills,
Bequeathing it as a rich legacy
Unto their issue.

FOURTH CITIZEN: We'll hear the will: read it, Mark
Antony.

ALL: The will, the will! We will hear
Caesar's will.

ANTONY: Have patience, gentle friends, I must
not read it;
It is not meet you know how Caesar
loved you.
You are not wood, you are not
stones, but men;
And, being men, bearing the will of
Caesar,
It will inflame you, it will make you
mad:
'Tis good you know not that you are
his heirs;
For, if you should, O, what would
come of it!

FOURTH CITIZEN: Read the will; we'll hear it, Antony;
You shall read us the will, Caesar's
will.

ANTONY: Will you be patient? Will you stay
awhile?

I have o'ershot myself to tell you of
it:
I fear I wrong the honourable men
Whose daggers have stabb'd Caesar;
I do fear it.

About to rush off to attack the conspirators, Antony strengthens
their resolve by reading to them the contents of the will. The effect
can be plainly seen:

ANTONY:            Here is the will, and under Caesar's
                   seal.
                   To every Roman citizen he gives,
                   To every several man, seventy-five
                   drachmas.
SECOND CITIZEN:    Most noble Caesar! We'll revenge
                   his death.
THIRD CITIZEN:     O royal Caesar!
ANTONY:            Hear me with patience.
ALL:               Peace, ho!
ANTONY:            Moreover, he hath left you all his
                   walks,
                   His private arbours and new-planted
                   orchards,
                   On this side of the Tiber; he hath
                   left them you,
                   And to your heirs for ever, common
                   pleasures,
                   To walk abroad, and recreate
                   yourselves.
                   Here was a Caesar! when comes
                   such another?

The audience, enraged, set off in search of Caesar's assassins.

He has clinched his case. Brutus and his fellow assassins have been undone. And so has the Roman Republic.

In the Forum – unmatched emotion destroys a republic. Photo: © Getty Images.

7

❧ ❧ ❧

On a technical level, successfully appealing to emotion is one of the orator's toughest tasks. Like anything in life its genuineness can be faked, and demagogues know how to counterfeit it on demand (the morality of this is discussed in the conclusion). It's also the orator's *most dangerous* task – which derives from what might be called 'the first law of *pathos*' for the orator, every emotion generates an equal and opposite emotional response. We saw this in the discussion above of Republican reactions to Barack Obama's oratory.

On 16 March 1968 Robert F. Kennedy announced his candidacy for the Democratic nomination for the US presidency. For the next 82 days – a story recounted brilliantly by the historian Thurston Clarke – 'Bobby' captured the imagination of voters across parties, races and classes with a frenzied campaign based not on television sound bites and attack-advertising but speeches to huge public rallies. He was assisted by excellent speechwriters, such as Adam Walinsky, Jeff Greenfield and occasionally Ted Sorensen, but necessity often required his stump speech to be thrown away and replaced by *extempore* remarks. While no political ingénue, Kennedy used these occasions to educate his audiences about the momentous issues facing America's fractured society in that troubled year: poverty, racism and the war in Vietnam. On every possible occasion he challenged the audience's smug views – whether it was telling college students that their draft deferral rights should be abolished, telling sober businessmen that they bore some of the responsibility for what was happening in Vietnam, and telling angry African Americans to stop rioting. To conservatives, these messages, combined with the frenzied reception he received from minorities and young people at his motorcades and rallies, made Kennedy appear a frighteningly radical demagogue. Bobby knew this and was well aware that in America in 1968, angry gunmen of the type who had murdered his brother five years before abounded. And in one of his finest moments – his reaction to the assassination of Martin Luther King, three weeks into his primary campaign, and only hours after the event, to a mainly black audience in Indianapolis, many of whose members were still unaware that King had just been declared dead – he called for another emotion: calm. Composed in his head in the car on the way to the rally and on the stage as it was being spoken, and made largely without reference to notes, the speech, with its appropriate *anaphora*, *polysyndeton* and *parallelism*, demonstrates once again the naturalness of rhetorical devices to practised and natural orators. It remains a model for intelligent public speech to candidates of all parties and beliefs, and a reminder that it's not necessary to talk at the level of the tabloids and talkback radio to connect with everyday people:

Ladies and Gentlemen.

I'm only going to talk to you just for a minute or so this evening, because I have some – some very sad news for all of you. Could you lower those signs, please? I have some very sad news for all of you, and, I think, sad news for all of our fellow citizens, and people who love peace all over the world; and that is that Martin Luther King was shot and was killed tonight in Memphis, Tennessee.

Martin Luther King dedicated his life to love and to justice between fellow human beings. He died in the cause of that effort. In this difficult day, in this difficult time for the United States, it's perhaps well to ask what kind of a nation we are and what direction we want to move in. For those of you who are black – considering the evidence evidently is that there were white people who were responsible – you can be filled with bitterness, and with hatred, and a desire for revenge.

We can move in that direction as a country, in greater polarization – black people amongst blacks, and white amongst whites, filled with hatred toward one another.

Or we can make an effort, as Martin Luther King did, to understand, and to comprehend, and replace that violence, that stain of bloodshed that has spread across our land, with an effort to understand, compassion, and love.

For those of you who are black and are tempted to fill with – be filled with hatred and mistrust of the injustice of such an

act, against all white people, I would only say that I can also
feel in my own heart the same kind of feeling. I had a
member of my family killed, but he was killed by a
white man.

But we have to make an effort in the United States. We
have to make an effort to understand, to get beyond, or go
beyond these rather difficult times.

My favourite . . . poet was Aeschylus. And he once wrote:

> Even in our sleep, pain which cannot forget
> falls drop by drop upon the heart,
> until, in our own despair,
> against our will,
> comes wisdom
> through the awful grace of God.

What we need in the United States is not division; what we
need in the United States is not hatred; what we need in the
United States is not violence and lawlessness, but is love,
and wisdom, and compassion toward one another, and a
feeling of justice toward those who still suffer within our
country, whether they be white or whether they be
black.

So I ask you tonight to return home, to say a prayer for the
family of Martin Luther King . . .

And let's dedicate ourselves to what the Greeks wrote so
many years ago: to tame the savageness of man and make
gentle the life of this world. Let us dedicate ourselves to
that, and say a prayer for our country and for our
people.

As Clarke relates, after the speech even the most radical black
militants listening knew the answer wasn't to attack the whites
in the mixed-race crowd or possibly even kill Kennedy himself as

Bobby Kennedy – inspiring hero to the Left, frightening demagogue to the Right. Photo: © Time & Life Pictures/Getty Images.

a representative of white society. The crowd broke up and went home, and Indianapolis, a city with a history of racial tensions, was the only major American city to escape riots as a result of Martin Luther King's assassination.

But Bobby couldn't calm the whole nation. Shortly after midnight on 5 June he was shot at close range by a deranged Palestinian-American named Sirhan Sirhan.

As Marvin Gaye's moving song 'Abraham, Martin and John', reminds us, four of the most emotive speakers in American history – Abraham Lincoln, Martin Luther King, John and Bobby Kennedy – were all assassinated. Brutus, Antony and Cicero also died violently – the latter in direct repayment for his oratory. Ronald Reagan escaped assassination through chance. Barack Obama had to make his election night address from behind a transparent bulletproof screen. If we are looking for our old friends Abraham, Martin, John and Bobby, their spirit lives on today

Has anybody seen our old friend Bobby? – Robert Kennedy's grave at Arlington National Cemetery. Photo: © Jarno Gonzalez Zarraonandia/Shutterstock.com.

in thoughtful and emotive speech, as martyrs to Cicero's conception of the ideal orator.

Potentially, stirring up audiences through grand, emotive oratory comes at a price, and the emotive speaker needs both extraordinary courage and something we discuss next: character.

# Chapter 6
# Character

## 1

—————————————— ☙ ☙ ☙ ——————————————

Two men are running for mayor of your city:

- **Candidate One** is a respected local doctor who runs a clinic providing free treatment to the families of local unemployed mill workers. He's been a tireless member of the local secondary school board, including five years as its president during which enrolments soared. Then there's his Congressional Medal of Honor, which he won as a medic in the first Iraq War by exposing himself to enemy fire to treat wounded infantrymen in no man's land. He's happily married and without a hint of personal or financial scandal. In fact, apart from reminding you that you're less than perfect by comparison, he has only one negative. He is the most *boring* speaker you have ever heard. As he moves ponderously through his now familiar stump speech, you find yourself losing interest in his policy ideas even though you've wished for them your whole life.

- **Candidate Two** is an amazing public speaker. He has the ability to electrify the huge crowds that pack the local town hall, employing rhetoric that moves you alternatively from tears of pity to fist-waving rage, and although you once opposed his policies, you find yourself joining in his refrain: 'Just do it'. Perhaps he's the agent of change the city really needs. But as you leave his rallies, you can't help but remember that unfortunate night he was arrested in a hotel room with that 15-year-old girl, and how at the trial the girl and her parents stunned the prosecution with their last-minute refusal to testify. Now, on the eve of the election, the local paper is reporting that the girl's outraged grandfather believes the parents were bribed by the candidate's attorney.

If, like most people, you end up voting for Candidate One, you've understood a crucial element of oratory: the character of the speaker – or what the Greeks called *ethos*. No amount of charm or logic will persuade the reasonable listener if the speaker is a known liar or suspected phoney or hasn't the strength of purpose to deliver what he or she promises.

# 2

The classical authorities rightly regarded the character of the speaker as one of the most important elements of a speech. As we have seen, Aristotle regarded *ethos* along with *pathos* and *logos* as one of the three forms of proof. As he tells us:

> We more readily and sooner believe reasonable men on all matters in general and absolutely on questions where precision is impossible and two views can be maintained.

Sadly, in a world in which information is multiplying, money can buy you the analysis you need, and citizens are drowning in facts and becoming increasingly bewildered, the credibility of the speaker is becoming increasingly important.

So how do we determine the character of the speaker? The classical authorities suggest three ways:

1. *Through the speaker's prior reputation.* In this view, virtuous character cannot be faked through the use of rhetorical devices; the audience already knows whether the speaker's claims and promises can be trusted.

2. *Through the speech itself.* The canny speaker will use rhetorical techniques to project a character that appeals to the particular audience. The speaker's aim is to inspire confidence in the speaker's common sense, virtue and goodwill towards the audience.

3. *By projecting the dominant values of the age.* Typically, the effective speaker appeals to the audience's belief in virtues like self-sacrifice, patriotism, bravery, humility, faith and egalitarianism.

In this chapter we will discuss the importance of character, using examples drawn mainly from recent US politics. Character is typically used by speakers from all nations, but nowhere is its use so pronounced as in the modern United States. This may be simply the result of a trend established fairly recently by the Kennedys and their speechwriters, but it seems likely to have something to do with that country's peculiar mixture of revolutionary idealism, religious sentimentalism and, perhaps more prosaically, the short attention span of television audiences – it's easier to believe something because you trust the speaker than to examine complex arguments. It may also be related to the survival of classical studies in American universities.

**3**

Character is central to US politics. One of its most acute observers, the journalist and novelist Joe Klein, believes that the Republican Party's exploitation of character and the Democratic Party's concentration on logical reasoning accounts in large part for the

Republicans' dominance of presidential elections from Reagan to Bush. (In fact, one could extend Klein's argument back to the Nixon era of the late 1960s and early 1970s.) Here's how Klein compares the two campaigning strategies:

- **Republican**: 'Voters had three basic questions about a candidate: Is he a strong leader? Can I trust him? Does he care about people like me? Politics was all about getting the public to answer "yes" to those three questions (of course an integral part of the job was aggressively – often stealthily and sometimes disgracefully – painting the opposition as weak, untrustworthy and effete).'
- **Democrat**: Strategists 'would take a poll to learn which issues people cared about – inevitably jobs, health care, education – and then the Dems would try to figure out the best ways to talk about those policies. They would use these abstractions – government initiatives! – to sell their candidate to a public that no longer trusted the government. The character of the candidate, they believed, would be inferred from the quality of his policies.'

As Klein adds, today presidential politics is all about character . . . or rather the appearance of character. The presentation of personality, not policy is the essence of campaigning.

And oratory has a big role to play in defining the character of candidates.

Anyone who has worked on a losing political campaign will immediately recognise the wisdom in Klein's analysis. Working as a policy adviser and speechwriter on the 2001 and 2004 Australian federal election campaigns, I was first astonished and then depressed by the contrasting efforts put into the production of policy statements by the major parties. For the entire year leading up to each election, the most highly qualified political aides working for my party – Labor – were absorbed in the production of policy documents of unmatched detail, accuracy and accounting precision on every subject imaginable. Hardly a single comma was out of place;

our costings were bulletproof. The major behind-the-scenes bustups of the campaigns involved what now seem absurdly trivial turf wars over whose policies got prominence. By contrast, the policy statements put out by our opponents – the conservative Coalition – appeared to be hastily cobbled-together afterthoughts. In both cases the conservatives won convincingly, largely because – likely following strategies learnt directly from the US Republicans – they were able to project their prime ministerial candidate as strong and decisive, and our candidates as, in turn, weak and dangerous.

In the most decisive loss in 2001, speech played a huge part. Having acted boldly (and some would argue heartlessly) to deny landing rights to refugee boats on the Australian coast, the conservative Prime Minister John Howard inserted this line (later found to have been based on the comments of a focus group participant) into his otherwise unremarkable election launch speech:

> *We* will decide who comes to this country and the
> circumstances in which they come.

Why was this sound bite – which dominated the campaign from that moment onwards – so devastating? For a start, the speechwriter's stylistic tricks from chapter 4 are on display: the repetition of 'come' at the end of each clause is *epiphora*; the disturbing antithesis of 'we' and 'they'; the meter – the first half *trochaic pentameter* and the second *iambic pentameter*. And while it's almost certain these devices were used unconsciously, this fact once again demonstrates Cicero's point that the rhythms of language are ultimately instinctive and their use makes a devastating line stand out from the rest of a speech – like that little girl's red coat in the black and white of Steven Spielberg's film *Schindler's List*.

Howard's line turned out to be far more effective than the many hundreds of pages of policy documents and speech transcripts published by the Opposition, because it projected the sorts of elements of character the majority of the audience – the electorate – wanted to hear (and which so disturbed the liberal minority): determination, strength and concern for 'us' (not them). Importantly, it was believable because it was consistent with what the audience knew about the speaker's prior character, which some describe as a belief in popular sovereignty, others xenophobia (making this another textbook example of *paradiastole*).

What the US Republican, and then the Australian Coalition Government, strategists had unwittingly done was rediscover the importance of character, which Aristotle, Cicero and others had recognised more than 2000 years before. In fact, the three questions about a candidate that Republicans had formulated to sell first Ronald Reagan and then the two Bushes to the American electorate correspond broadly to the three qualities Aristotle and the classical theorists who followed him had identified as necessary for the successful establishment of character.

**Classical and modern qualities for the establishment of character**

| Aristotle's components of character | The Republicans' questions |
| --- | --- |
| virtue, courage, strength (*arete*) | Is he a strong leader? |
| common sense, practical wisdom (*phronesis*) | Can I trust him? |
| goodwill towards the audience (*eunoia*) | Does he care about people like me? |

How does a speaker go about establishing his or her good character to their audience? As we saw in section 2 above, there are three ways: through the speaker's prior reputation, through the speech itself, and by projecting the dominant values of the age.

# 4

Let's start with prior reputation. Often, the speaker's character has been on public display and has been established by prior deeds, not words. This is the case in our fictional election contest, where the prior reputations of the speakers are decisive – one a war hero, the other a ruthless cad. There are few occasions, however, when the gulf between two opposing speakers' characters is as wide and obvious as between Candidate One and Candidate Two. Occasionally, though, something approaching it does happen in reality.

Since the rebirth of American oratory in the early 1960s – the result of the fortunate coincidence of great speechwriters like Ted Sorensen and Peggy Noonan and gifted speakers like the Kennedys and Ronald Reagan – that country has not been short of magisterial orators. One of the best, able to move the faithful like few others, was the youngest of the Kennedy brothers, Edward. Many great speakers are remembered for one speech, but Teddy Kennedy is remembered for two.

The first is the eulogy (and therefore an example of display rhetoric) he delivered on 8 June 1968 for his second slain brother, Bobby, the most memorable passage of which is here:

> My brother need not be idealised, or enlarged in death
> beyond what he was in life; to be remembered simply as a
> good and decent man, who saw wrong and tried to right it,
> saw suffering and tried to heal it, saw war and tried to
> stop it.

> Those of us who loved him and who take him to his rest
> today, pray that what he was to us and what he wished for
> others will some day come to pass for all the world. As he
> said many times, in many parts of this nation, to those he
> touched and who sought to touch him: 'Some men see
> things as they are and say "why". I dream things that never
> were and say "why not".'

The speech-craft is obvious: in the first paragraph a *tricolon* featuring *anaphora*, *epiphora*, *parison* and *asyndeton*. In the second, also examples of *parallelism* ('what he was to us and what he wished for others'; 'those he touched and sought to touch him'); a notable set of *antithesis* ('some men' versus 'I', 'see' versus 'dream', 'things as they are' versus 'things that never were', 'say why' versus 'say why not' – the use of 'why' here also being a *polyploton*); and meter (*iambic pentameter*). But it is also in itself a textbook use of *ethos* through its appeal to the values of the audience (righting wrong, healing suffering, making peace, dreaming of a better world).

The second, delivered on 12 August 1980, was his speech to the 1980 Democratic National Convention. After appealing to the issues and emotions dear to the left and blue-collar wings of his party who supported the family cause, Kennedy ended with the following lines, which were penned by the speechwriter and later campaign consultant Bob Shrum:

> Someday, long after this convention, long after the signs come down and the crowds stop cheering, and the bands stop playing, may it be said of our campaign that we kept the faith.
>
> May it be said of our Party that we found our faith again.
>
> And may it be said of us, both in dark passages and in bright days, in the words of Tennyson that my brothers quoted and loved, and that have special meaning for me now:
>
>> I am a part of all that I have met . . .
>> Tho' much is taken, much abides . . .
>> [To] which we are, we are –
>> One equal temper of heroic hearts . . . strong in will
>> To strive, to seek, to find, and not to yield.
>
> For me, a few hours ago, this campaign came to an end. For all those whose cares have been our concern, the work goes on, the cause endures, the hope still lives, and the dream shall never die.

Again this speech contains impressive speech-craft – most notably in the third and last paragraphs with their obvious *anaphora* and *polysyndeton* – but also examples of *ethos* in the explicit appeals to faith, hopes, dreams and the classical heroism of Tennyson's Greek warrior Ulysses. This appeal to character was a hallmark of the Kennedy style, but it was also something Teddy Kennedy in particular needed, because it was his Achilles heel. After the tragic and heroic deaths of his brothers, possessing enormous wealth, bathed in the aura of American 'royalty', and blessed with the oratorical skills to inspire Democrats and carry Democratic Conventions, the stage was set for the youngest Kennedy to become president at the end of the Nixon era. It should have been Teddy, not Jimmy Carter.

Then, on the evening of 18 July 1969, after a party in honour of his late brother Robert's former campaign staff, he drove his car off the Dike Bridge on Chappaquiddick Island, and left the scene of the accident, in which his passenger, Mary Jo Kopechne, drowned. Despite claiming to have made numerous attempts to save Kopechne, and despite no indictment being issued by a grand jury, the judge at the inquest into the incident concluded that parts of Kennedy's story could not be believed. So for the rest of his career, Kennedy was dogged by the suspicion that he was a philanderer, had been drunk at the wheel, had left a young girl to drown, had broken the law and had lied to authorities. Teddy Kennedy failed the character test, and whether or not the suspicions were true, he was never able to overcome the damage to his reputation. The guaranteed Democratic victory after the Watergate scandal was not to be his. During the 1980 primary campaign, which ended with the second of the speeches above, he was subjected to the taunts of demonstrators asking 'Where is Mary Jo?'

## 5

Sometimes someone's perceived bad character seems less deserved. A good example of this was the fate of the Democratic presidential nominee in 2004, John Kerry. Kerry's supposed strength as a candidate was his record as a decorated veteran in Vietnam, who famously exposed himself to enemy fire to rescue his troops as commander of a swift boat on the Mekong Delta. Like Candidate One, this should have made him a shoo-in for the election. But Kerry had also just as famously been a leader of the Vietnam War protest movement – and as a senator was sometimes indecisive.

If the Republicans were to beat him in an electoral atmosphere still influenced by the 9/11 terrorist attacks, they had to destroy his character as a patriot. A group called Swift Boat Veterans for Truth, which had strongly suspected links to the Republican Party, proceeded to undermine Kerry's account of his wartime record. And the Republicans used every opportunity to paint Kerry as unpatriotic and indecisive. At the Republican National Convention in New York in September 2004 vice-presidential candidate Dick Cheney and turncoat Democratic senator Zell Miller used their keynote addresses to flay Kerry.

Here's Miller, speaking on 1 September 2004, using a wide variety of the speechwriter's standard rhetorical tools to add to the speech's destructive force.

---

**Rhetorical tools used to add a speech's destructive force**

| | |
|---|---|
| No one should dare to even think about being the Commander in Chief of this country if he doesn't believe with all his heart that our soldiers are liberators abroad and defenders of freedom at home. | *Maxim* |
| But don't waste your breath telling that to the leaders of my party today. In their warped way of thinking, America is the problem, not the solution. They don't believe there is any real danger in the world except that which America brings upon itself through our clumsy and misguided foreign policy.<br>It is not their patriotism; it is their judgement that has been so sorely lacking. | *Paralipsis* – Miller pretends not to be drawing attention to Kerry's lack of patriotism but it is his prime objective (see below his reference to 'as a war protester'.) |
| They claimed Carter's pacifism would lead to peace. They were wrong.<br>They claimed Reagan's defence build up would lead to war. They were wrong.<br>And no pair has been more wrong, more loudly, more often than the two Senators from Massachusetts, Ted Kennedy and John Kerry. | *Anaphora* – 'They claimed'<br>*Epiphora* – 'They were wrong.'<br>*Anaphora* and *tricolon* – 'more' |

(cont.)

**Rhetorical tools used to add a speech's destructive force (*cont.*)**

| | |
|---|---|
| Together, Kennedy and Kerry have opposed the very weapons system that won the Cold War and that are now winning the war on terror. | *Simile* – Kerry likened to conservative bogeyman Ted Kennedy<br>*Repetition* – 'war' |
| The B-1 bomber, that Senator Kerry opposed, dropped 40 per cent of the bombs in the first six months of Enduring Freedom.<br>The B-2 bomber, that Senator Kerry opposed, delivered air strikes against the Taliban in Afghanistan and Hussein's command post in Iraq.<br>The F-14A Tomcats, that Senator Kerry opposed, shot down Gadhafi's Libyan MiGs over the Gulf of Sidra.<br>The modernised F-14D, that Senator Kerry opposed, delivered missile strikes against Tora Bora.<br>The Apache helicopter, that Senator Kerry opposed, took out those Republican Guard tanks in Kuwait in the Gulf War.<br>The F-15 Eagles, that Senator Kerry opposed, flew cover over our nation's capital and this very city after 9/11. | *Anaphora* – 'The ... that Senator Kerry opposed ...' |
| I could go on and on and on ... against the Patriot Missile that shot down Saddam Hussein's scud missiles over Israel; against the Aegis air-defence cruiser; against the Strategic Defence Initiative; against the Trident missile, against, against, against. | *Anaphora* – 'against'<br>*Ellipsis* – omission of what he's also against (it seems everything ...) |
| This is the man who wants to be the Commander in Chief of our US Armed Forces? US forces armed with what? Spit balls? | *Erotema* – 'armed with what?'<br>*Sarcasm* and *hyperbole* – 'Spit balls.' |
| For more than 20 years, on every one of the great issues of freedom and security, John Kerry has been more wrong, more weak and more wobbly than any other national figure. | *Anaphora* – 'more'. |

Character references don't come more negative than that. But as millions of Americans thought at the time, why didn't Kerry fight back by pointing out that the very people accusing him of being unpatriotic had themselves managed to find ways of avoiding being drafted to fight in Vietnam? As Klein says, who could believe John Kerry would make a strong president, when he didn't have the strength of character to stand up and defend his own good name? A great speech about the boys he saved in Vietnam – and the ones George W. Bush didn't – might have helped, but it was never made.

Someone who was prepared to stand up for his and others' characters in the face of considerable political danger was Joseph Welch, chief legal counsel for the Army in the infamous Army–McCarthy hearings. Senator Joseph McCarthy had made his name by destroying the reputations of others through exposing their supposed past associations with the Communist Party. On 9 June 1954 Welch responded to a claim by McCarthy that a junior counsel at Welch's law form, Fred Fisher, had past communist connections:

> Until this moment, Senator, I think I never gauged your
> cruelty or your recklessness . . . Let us not assassinate this
> lad further, Senator. You've done enough. Have you no
> sense of decency, sir, at long last? Have you left no sense
> of decency?

The public galleries applauded enthusiastically. McCarthy, until this time seemingly immune from criticism, had been humiliated and exposed as cruel and arrogant. His character impugned, it was the beginning of the end. Broken, he died an alcoholic three years later at the age of just 48.

Kerry's campaign and Welch's destruction of McCarthy proved that in politics you have to establish and defend your own character or your enemies will do it for you. And the best way to do it is in a speech.

## 6

🐿 🐿 🐿

While we generally have some idea of the character of the speakers
to whom we listen – especially if they are famous – the smart
speaker seldom leaves this to chance. Hence the second way of
expressing *ethos*: the use of techniques to project the speaker's
positive qualities. We've seen how John Kerry neglected this and
paid the price. He was far from the first speaker to fail in this
fundamental task; in fact he could have learnt a lot from the failure
of his immediate predecessor as Democratic presidential nominee,
Al Gore.

Gore's candidacy for the 2000 presidential race is generally
regarded as a disaster. It's a race he should have won but didn't
because he was unable to project any sort of attractive personality. Again, as Klein puts it: 'He lost the election – actually it was
a dead heat – because he did not seem a credible human being'.
Gore's public performances were described as wooden, plastic and
dull. Like the candidates I worked for, he had the more convincing policies, but the Republicans' three big questions still went
unanswered. Gore's attempts to project decisiveness and human
qualities by showing more aggression in the televised debates failed
miserably. The celebrity feminist theorist Naomi Wolf was even
hired to advise him on his personal style, and it was claimed
that she told him to wear 'earth tones' and behave more as an
'alpha male'. Whether that was true or not, the fact that such
rumours circulated so freely in the national press demonstrated that
everyone was aware that Gore had a major problem projecting a
strong character.

But Gore learnt from his failures.

Gore has managed to resurrect his reputation, becoming the
generally acknowledged leader of the worldwide campaign to
prevent global warming. And he chose to do it through speech.

After losing the 2000 presidential race, Gore returned to doing
what he does best – touring the world convincing audiences of
the need to reduce greenhouse gas emissions. By his own claim,

he had delivered his PowerPoint presentation approximately 1000 times, perfecting it until in 2004 it was seen by Hollywood producer Lawrence Bender and environmental activist Laurie David, who realised its potential to become an important documentary film, and put Gore in touch with film-maker Davis Guggenheim. The result was an amazing success that not only won two Academy Awards but has also been credited with re-energising what by 2006 had become a flagging world environmental movement. But *An Inconvenient Truth* is not just a movie; it's a movie adaptation of an extraordinarily powerful and intelligently formulated piece of oratory. Its success can be put down to a number of factors – including good timing and the fact that like all great speeches it employs many of the rhetorical techniques that had been identified by classical theorists of oratory more than 2000 years ago. This makes *An Inconvenient Truth* a modern equivalent of Cicero with a PowerPoint projector. (And if the scientific claims it makes are indeed true, it may turn out to be many times more important than any speech made by Cicero himself.)

You don't have to agree with Gore's presentation to recognise its effective use of persuasive techniques – something acknowledged through a backhanded compliment by those who devoted so much time to criticising it as 'pure rhetoric'. We will be referring to *An Inconvenient Truth* in chapter 7 to illustrate the film's effective use of evidence, but for the moment let's focus on its use of character, because it's a key element of the movie's appeal. Gore does this in three major interventions in his presentation.

---

**Use of character in *An Inconvenient Truth***

---

**1 Hero**

| | |
|---|---|
| This [picture of Earth from outer space] is the image that started me in my interest in this issue. I saw it when I was a college student because I had a college professor named Roger Revelle | Gore uses a discussion of the origins of climate science to tell a story about his long-term association with the professor who helped begin his serious scientific study of global warming. |

*(cont.)*

CHARACTER

**167**

who was the first person to have the idea to measure the amount of carbon dioxide in the Earth's atmosphere. He saw where the story was going. After the first few years of data, he intuited what is meant, for what is yet to come...

It was a wonderful time for me, because, like a lot of young people, I came into contact with intellectual ferment, ideas that I'd never considered in my wildest dreams before.

He showed our class the result of these measurements after only a few years. It was startling to me. He was startled and he made it clear to our class what he felt the significance of it was. I soaked it up like a sponge. He drew the connection between the larger changes in our civilisation and this pattern that was now visible in the atmosphere entire planet.

He projected into the future where this was headed unless we made some adjustments and it was as clear as day...

I respected him and learned from him so much...

When I went to the Congress in the middle 1970s I helped organise the first hearings on global warming, I asked my professor to be the lead off witness. I thought that would have such a big impact we'd be well on the way to solving this problem, but it didn't work out that way. I kept having

From the way this is done, we learn much about speaker that is admirable:

- he is someone who respects mentors
- the mentor provides a moment of revelation that demonstrates these beliefs are deeply held
- he is no Johnny-come-lately to this cause – it is a life-long passion
- he has taken up the cause as his own and acted upon it consistently and honestly where others have not.

As storytellers and Hollywood scriptwriters have long recognised, the progression from (1) innocence, to (2) meeting a mentor, to (3) revelation, to (4) crusade, is the journey of the hero. Gore has managed brilliantly to take potentially dull science and use it to project himself as a hero on a quest.

hearings, and in 1984 I went to the Senate and really dug deeply into this issue with science round tables and the like. I wrote a book about it. I ran for president in 1988 partly try to gain some visibility for this issue. In 1992 I went to the White House. We passed a version of [a] carbon tax and some other measures to try to address this. I went to Kyoto in 1997 to help get a treaty that is so controversial, in the US at least. In 2000 my opponent pledged to regulate the $CO_2$ and that was not a pledge that was kept.

## 2 Father

April 3, 1989. My son pulled loose from my hand and chased his friend across the street. He was six years old.

[Hospital scenes] The machine was breathing for him. We were possibly going to lose him. He finally took a breath.

We stayed in the hospital for a month. It was almost as if you could look at that calendar and just go...

And everything just flew off. Seemed trivial, insignificant.

He was so brave. He was such... He was such a brave guy.

It just turned my whole world upside down and then shook it until everything fell out. My way of being in the world, it just changed everything for me. How should I spend my time on this Earth?

This section of Gore's speech explains what's at stake in the fight against global warming: a future for our children.

By telling the story of the near-death of his son, Gore throws off the image of the earnest policy wonk to show he's just like us and is inspired by ordinary human emotions. As loving parents ourselves, Gore's quest to protect his children is one we feel compelled to emulate.

It's Gore as the thing he wasn't as a presidential candidate: a credible human being.

CHARACTER

**169**

(*cont.*)

I really dug in, trying to learn about it much more deeply. I went to Antarctica. Went to the South Pole, the North Pole, the Amazon. Went to places where scientists could help me understand parts of the issue that I didn't really understand in depth.

The possibility of losing what was most precious to me. I gained an ability that maybe I didn't have before. But when I felt it, I felt that we could really lose it, that what we take for granted might not be here for our children.

### 3 Brother

I don't remember a time when I was a kid when summertime didn't mean working with tobacco. I used to love it. It was during that period when working with the guys on the farm seemed like fun to me.

Starting in 1964 with the Surgeon General's report, the evidence was laid out on the connection between smoking cigarettes and lung cancer. We kept growing tobacco.

Nancy was almost 10 years older than me, and there were only two of us. She was my protector and my friend at the same time. She started smoking when she was a teenager and never stopped. She died of lung cancer. That's one of the ways you don't want to die.

Gore wants to find a *metaphor* to explain how climate change deniers use doubt to undermine the findings of climate science – he finds it in the actions of the tobacco industry. This is made more powerful by the fact that his own family were tobacco growers and that his only and much-loved sister died from smoking-related lung cancer.

This story allows Gore to make the further point that we need to learn to join the dots between our economic actions and their very real moral consequences.

As with the story of his son's accident, this provides the audience with a back story: Gore as the happy child growing up on a farm; the loved and loving brother; someone who shares complicity but has seen the light; who feels a sense of

The idea that we had been part of that economic pattern that produced the cigarettes that produced the cancer, it was so painful at so many levels. My father, he had grown tobacco all his life. He stopped it. Whatever explanation that seemed to make sense in the past, just didn't cut it anymore. He stopped it.

It's just human nature to take time to connect the dots. I know that. But I also know that there can be a day of reckoning when you wished you had connected the dots more quickly.

tragic responsibility and who wants to get even with scientific deniers. Like Captain Ahab's pursuit of the great white whale, this is personal! It's a classic Hollywood story.

Al Gore – hero, brother, father. Photo: © stocklight/Shutterstock.com.

The film-makers who gave us the screen version of Gore's stump speech knew full well the huge problem represented by his dull public persona. Even though Laurie David described it as 'the most powerful and clear explanation of global warming' she had ever seen, the presentation needed a lot of work to reach beyond the comparatively small number of true believers to become a box office hit. They knew that until they could make the speaker an appealing figure, the project was doomed.

Here's what the director Davis Guggenheim had to say:

> I felt it was critical to add the personal narrative in the film, and he [Gore] was not so sure about that. I mean, he wasn't sure why we would need to go back and talk about his son's accident and how he learned from it, and I thought it was a critical element for people to hook in to the movie. The feeling was that if the audience invested in him, in his journey to tell the story and trying to ring this alarm bell, that if we did that, then audiences would hook in emotionally to what is a very abstract and scientific issue.

In other words, and as Aristotle would have recognised, they needed to project Gore's character to give his proof greater force. They succeeded spectacularly. Despite this, the cynical obviously reject Gore's use of his personal journey to increase the persuasiveness of his presentation. In a university symposium, where the science is being tested by the presenter's peers, they would have a point. But in the court of public opinion (where, incidentally, audience members are also free to assess afterwards the validity of the science presented) there is no pay off for failing to engage an audience or convince it that the speaker is sincere and trustworthy.

As one would expect, Gore's enemies have ridiculed him for this use of character and emotion to help make his point, but they haven't been the only ones. Leading climate change scientists and environmental economists also occasionally snigger about Gore's presentation, believing it to be counter-productive and embarrass-ing – something I've witnessed personally. In 2008, I was engaged by a public relations agent to brighten up the stump presentation of a leading climate change advocate (whose speeches, unlike his sharp, clear prose, were unrelentingly tedious). However, my attempts were bluntly rejected by his advisers who believed that the science must speak for itself. The effectiveness of their faith in logic alone to carry the day was demonstrated when the speaker's final report proved to be so detailed and complex, and his presentation of it so uninspiring and convoluted, that it contributed to the draining of momentum from the issue. The pure, as they say, are impotent and sometimes uninspiring.

We've seen how the great conservative cause of the twentieth century, defeating communism, was conquered in part because of the stirring rhetoric of people such as John F. Kennedy and Ronald Reagan. The first great liberal cause of the twenty-first century, climate change, succeeded in gaining momentum largely because Al Gore and the people who made a movie of his stump speech also understood that facts alone were not enough, and that the facts had to be matched with emotion and character. They knew they had to stand toe to toe in the forum with their opponents. Cicero would have approved.

# 7

 ❧ ❧ ❧

While Teddy Kennedy was unable to embody personally the *ethos* of his speeches, his brother John F. Kennedy had no such problem. By the time he stood successfully for president, Kennedy's character as a war hero and articulate intellectual was well known and carefully cultivated through his early speeches and (partly ghost-written) books, and this was used to appeal to a youthful generation of idealistic voters through magisterial speeches written with the help of Ted Sorensen. (This is another task the speechwriter will be asked to assume – ghost writer of his or her clients' books.) Kennedy made a number of these speeches, which used the idea of sacrifice as their central motif. Take, for instance, his justification for the Apollo program to land a man on the Moon, in his address to the students of Rice University on 12 September 1962, with its nicely rendered use of *anaphora* and *antithesis*:

We choose to go to the Moon. We choose to go to the
Moon in this decade and do the other things, not because
they are easy, but because they are hard, because that goal
will serve to organise and measure the best of our energies
and skills, because that challenge is one that we are willing
to accept, one we are unwilling to postpone, and one which
we intend to win.

It would have been easy for Kennedy to give the hard-headed
reason – to get there before the Soviets – but as he often did he
tried to appeal to what Lincoln called the audience's better angels:
because it is hard; because it tests our character!

Kennedy's most famous example of the use of *ethos* was his inaugural address on 20 January 1961. Regarded as one of the greatest
presidential speeches of the twentieth century, it was primarily
authored by Sorensen, but included input from others, including
John Kenneth Galbraith, Arthur Schlesinger Jr., Adlai Stephenson
and Walter Lippmann. Its intentional Lincolnesque style (Kennedy
had told Sorensen to read Lincoln for inspiration) set the standard
for Kennedy's later speeches, and this neo-Lincolnism has influenced presidential speeches ever since.

---

**John F. Kennedy's inaugural address**

---

| | |
|---|---|
| Let the word go forth from this time and place, to friend and foe alike, that the torch has been passed to a new generation of Americans – born in this century, tempered by war, disciplined by a hard and bitter peace, proud of our ancient heritage – and unwilling to witness or permit the slow undoing of those human rights to which this nation has always been committed, and to which we are committed today at home and around the world. | Call to a new generation to take up the revolutionary cause |

**John F. Kennedy's inaugural address (*cont.*)**

| | |
|---|---|
| Let every nation know, whether it wishes us well or ill, that we shall pay any price, bear any burden, meet any hardship, support any friend, oppose any foe, in order to assure the survival and the success of liberty. | The famous call to sacrifice, which stands out because it uses *asyndeton* and *parison* |
| In your hands, my fellow citizens, more than in mine, will rest the final success or failure of our course. Since this country was founded, each generation of Americans has been summoned to give testimony to its national loyalty. The graves of young Americans who answered the call to service surround the globe.<br>Now the trumpet summons us again...<br>Can we forge against these enemies a grand and global alliance, North and South, East and West, that can assure a more fruitful life for all mankind? Will you join in that historic effort? | The appeal to emulate the fallen |
| In the long history of the world, only a few generations have been granted the role of defending freedom in its hour of maximum danger. I do not shrink from this responsibility – I welcome it. I do not believe that any of us would exchange places with any other people or any other generation. The energy, the faith, the devotion which we bring to this endeavour will light our country and all who serve it – and the glow from that fire can truly light the world. | The acceptance of responsibility<br>The use of energy, faith and devotion<br>The metaphorical religious call to be the light of the world |

(*cont.*)

CHARACTER

And so, my fellow Americans: ask not what your country can do for you – ask what you can do for your country.

My fellow citizens of the world: ask not what America will do for you, but what together we can do for the freedom of man.

The patriotic call to duty, which, thanks to its use of *antimetabole*, is perhaps the most famous political sentence of the twentieth century.

John F. Kennedy famously asks 'not what...' Photo: © Time & Life Pictures/Getty Images.

The writers of *The West Wing* were masters of employing *ethos* to appeal to liberals – something their conservative contemporaries actually managed to do better in real life. Character is central to the program's appeal, and at times the characters seem to be channelling John F. Kennedy's call to sacrifice and service – particularly in the show's set piece speeches. One of the best is the speech made by the fictional Democratic primary contender Matt Santos – a man who has all the positive aspects of our Candidate One combined with the sublime public-speaking gifts of the Kennedys. At the end of series six, Santos makes a speech that steals the nomination in a brokered Democratic National Convention by projecting character and idealism (and showing considerable *extempore* rhetorical technique):

> It has been suggested to me this week that I should try to buy your support with jobs and the promise of access. It's been suggested to me that party unity is more important than your democratic rights as delegates. [AUDIENCE ROARS] That's right, it's not. And you have a decision to make. Don't vote for us because you think we're perfect. Don't vote for us because of what we might be able to do for you only. Vote for the person who shares your ideals, your hopes, your dreams. Vote for the person who most embodies what you believe we need to keep our nation strong and free. And when you've done that you can go back . . . with your head held high and say 'I am a member of the Democratic Party'.

There is more than a faint echo of 'ask not' in this speech. It's little wonder that many believe that the enormous appeal of the program's characters to liberal Americans paved the way for a Santos-like primary contender to become the real-life occupant of the West Wing.

## 8

Kennedy's and Santos' use of character was grandiloquent – what Cicero would call the grand style – calling for idealism and self-sacrifice. But this isn't the only way to express the third meaning of *ethos*. The other way is through *empathy* – identifying not with

Jimmy Smits as Matt Santos in *The West Wing* channels the Kennedys and inspires Obama. Photo: © Warner Bros./Getty Images.

the noble ideals of the audience but their everyday concerns and humble circumstances, to answer the question, 'Does the speaker care about me?' And this often involves trying to sound down-to-earth.

This is easier than it looks, and often provides a great way to open a speech and introduce its themes. When, for instance, the Secretary to the Australian Department of Treasury wanted to make a keynote address on the potentially boring topic of tax reform in 2008, his department was looking for a way of making the subject matter interesting to the journalists in the room and the television viewers at home. Having remembered Dr Ken Henry's ability in previous speeches to talk warmly and convincingly about his life, I suggested he think of an episode where taxpayers had related their negative experiences of the existing tax system to him. The end product, largely the work of Henry himself, was well received, bringing out his idealism as a (practical) conservationist, his lack of cosmopolitan airs and graces, his ability to mix with ordinary people, and his sense of humour. (To the insiders in the room it was also an allusion to the fact that this was the first holiday the nation's hardest working and most important public servant had taken in a long, long time.) They already knew he was smart; now, knowing he was a listener and hard worker, the audience was more prepared to hear him out:

> As people all around the world quickly learned – such is the reach of the electronic media these days – I spent July with my wife, Naomi, in the Epping Forest Scientific National Park in central Queensland, helping look after what may be the last 115 northern hairy-nosed wombats left on the planet . . .
>
> On the first night of our trip home from Epping Forest, Naomi and I stopped at Jericho, a small town to the south-west of the park. While waiting for dinner – it was Thursday pizza night at the pub – we sat in the bar for a drink. A local businessman, let's call him Jim, came up to have a chat . . .
>
> 'So, what do you do for a living?' he asked. I was going to say 'I'm a wildlife protection officer', which was sort of true. But I said: 'I work for government, in Canberra'. Perhaps I sounded a bit defensive – I didn't mean to – because he responded: 'That's all right mate, somebody has to'. And then he added, 'Just so long as you don't have anything to do with tax.'
>
> Well, discretion is part of my job description. Even so, we ended up having a long and – I think – insightful discussion about the complexities of the tax system that ordinary Australians have to deal with.

As well as down-to-earth, projecting character can also involve try-ing to sound intentionally inarticulate and tongue-tied. This is some-thing contemporary American politicians are also good at.

A potentially boring speech about taxation succeeds in getting people to listen and think. The lesson for the speechwriter is simple: only connect.

# 9

ᴙ ᴙ ᴙ

In some ways the fight over this form of character – *empathy* – is what has been at the heart of American politics since the Nixon years, when conservatives began to paint their liberal opponents as out-of-touch elites in an attempt to steal the Southern and blue-collar base that had sustained the Democratic Party since the presidency of Franklin Delano Roosevelt. A similar style of politics has been played out in most other parts of the democratic world. As we've seen, Democrats like John Kerry failed spectacularly to counter it. If any person was susceptible to this strategy it was the Harvard educated, African-American Barack Obama. And both the Democrats and Republicans knew it. So let's return to Obama's and Palin's Convention speeches to see how they used these techniques.

In the lead up to the election, the Republicans had attempted to bracket Obama as a typical out-of-touch north-eastern liberal: he had never run a business or served in the military, but had managed to achieve success through political celebrity. While the Republican candidates couldn't raise the race issue directly, others weren't so scrupulous. The Democratic candidate had to use his Convention speech to re-define himself as typically American.

---

**Barak Obama's use of character in his 2008 Convention speech**

| | |
|---|---|
| ...to the next vice president of the United States, Joe Biden, I thank you. [APPLAUSE] <br> I am grateful to finish this journey with one of the finest statesmen of our time, a man at ease with everyone from world leaders to the conductors on the Amtrak train he still takes home every night. | Vice-Presidential running mate Joseph Biden's working-class credentials are used to associate Obama with blue-collar America. |
| To the love of my life, our next first lady, Michelle Obama, [APPLAUSE] | Husband and father |

and to Malia and Sasha – I love you so much, and I am so proud of you. [APPLAUSE]

Four years ago, I stood before you and told you my story, of the brief union between a young man from Kenya and a young woman from Kansas who weren't well-off or well-known, but shared a belief that in America their son could achieve whatever he put his mind to.

Obama's mixed-race heritage and part-Muslim background and middle name – potential electoral negatives highlighted remorselessly by his opponents – are re-defined to identify him with soldiers and hard-working middle America.

It is that promise that's always set this country apart, that through hard work and sacrifice each of us can pursue our individual dreams, but still come together as one American family, to ensure that the next generation can pursue their dreams as well. That's why I stand here tonight. Because for 232 years, at each moment when that promise was in jeopardy, ordinary men and women – students and soldiers, farmers and teachers, nurses and janitors – found the courage to keep it alive...

And when one of his [McCain's] chief advisers, the man who wrote his economic plan, was talking about the anxieties that Americans are feeling, he said that we were just suffering from a mental recession and that we've become, and I quote, 'a nation of whiners.' [AUDIENCE BOOS]

Obama identifies with the ordinary people against the out-of-touch Republican elites – turning the tables on a favoured Republican tactic.

Inciting anger by referring to the description of Americans as 'whiners' is a textbook case also of *pathos*.

A nation of whiners? Tell that to the proud auto workers at a Michigan plant who, after they found out it was closing, kept showing up every day and working as hard as

(*cont.*)

ever, because they knew there
were people who counted on the
brakes that they made.
Tell that to the military families who
shoulder their burdens silently as
they watch their loved ones leave
for their third, or fourth, or fifth
tour of duty.
These are not whiners. They work
hard, and they give back, and they
keep going without complaint.
These are the Americans I know...
[APPLAUSE]

Because in the faces of those young
veterans who come back from Iraq
and Afghanistan, I see my
grandfather, who signed up after
Pearl Harbor, marched in Patton's
army, and was rewarded by a
grateful nation with the chance to
go to college on the G.I. Bill.
In the face of that young student,
who sleeps just three hours before
working the night shift, I think
about my mom, who raised my
sister and me on her own while
she worked and earned her degree,
who once turned to food stamps,
but was still able to send us to
the best schools in the country
with the help of student loans and
scholarships. [APPLAUSE]
When I listen to another worker tell
me that his factory has shut down,
I remember all those men and
women on the South Side of
Chicago who I stood by and
fought for two decades ago after
the local steel plant closed.
And when I hear a woman talk
about the difficulties of starting her
own business or making her way

Obama counters the
Republican claim that he's
an Ivy League-educated
celebrity candidate by
turning his successes into
the hard-won achievement of
a typical American family.
He may not have served in
the armed forces, but his
grandfather fought with
Patton.

in the world, I think about my grandmother, who worked her way up from the secretarial pool to middle management, despite years of being passed over for promotions because she was a woman.

She's the one who taught me about hard work. She's the one who put off buying a new car or a new dress for herself so that I could have a better life. She poured everything she had into me. And although she can no longer travel, I know that she's watching tonight and that tonight is her night, as well. [APPLAUSE]

Now, I don't know what kind of lives John McCain thinks that celebrities lead, but this has been mine.

Barack Obama – grandfather marched in Patton's army. Photo: © Frontpage/Shutterstock.com.

When Sarah Palin rose to give her convention speech a week later, the Republican attack on Obama's character continued. As second on the Republican ticket, and from the right of her party, Palin would have been expected to play bad cop to McCain's good cop. But as a largely unknown, and someone eager to establish her own independent profile, Palin also set out to establish her own story and character – which she did through a brilliant empathetic appeal to the patriotic values of small-town middle America.

We've seen already in chapter 5 how Sarah Palin used the *pathos* of John McCain's personal story to highlight his character as well. So let's examine how she uses *ethos* to make a case for her own cause.

---

**Sarah Palin's use of *ethos* in her 2008 Republican Convention Speech**

---

Our nominee for president is a true profile in courage, and people like that are hard to come by. He's a man who wore the uniform of his country for 22 years and refused to break faith with those troops in Iraq who now have brought victory within sight. [APPLAUSE]

And as the mother of one of those troops, that is exactly the kind of man I want as commander in chief. [APPLAUSE]

I'm just one of many moms who will say an extra prayer each night for our sons and daughters going into harm's way. Our son, Track, is 19. And one week from tomorrow – September 11th – he'll deploy to Iraq with the Army infantry in the service of his country.

My nephew, Kasey, also enlisted and serves on a carrier in the Persian Gulf.

My family is proud of both of them and of all the fine men and women serving the country in uniform.

Palin segues from describing McCain's military record to describe that of her own family. She has a personal stake in America's military deployments. This *trope* – of the patriotic but long-suffering mother in a time of war – goes back to the time of Homer and the plays of Euripides.

*Praeteritio* is used to imply that the Democratic candidate is not proud of America's servicemen and women.

## Sarah Palin's use of *ethos* in her 2008 Republican Convention Speech (*cont.*)

[APPLAUSE] [AUDIENCE: 'USA! USA! USA! USA! USA!']

| | |
|---|---|
| Track is the eldest of our five children. In our family, it's two boys and three girls in between, my strong and kind-hearted daughters, Bristol, and Willow and Piper. [APPLAUSE] | Palin tries to establish empathy by posing as a typical mother and grandmother. |
| And we were so blessed in April. Todd and I welcomed our littlest one into the world, a perfectly beautiful baby boy named Trig. | *Pathos* and *praeteritio* are used here as Palin's 'perfectly beautiful baby' has Down syndrome. |
| You know, from the inside, no family ever seems typical, and that's how it is with us. Our family has the same ups and downs as any other, the same challenges and the same joys. | *Litotes* – the audience (and the whole nation) knows that despite her profession of strong Bible-truth Christian ethics, her first grandchild is the result of pre-marital sex by her 18-year-old eldest daughter. |
| Sometimes even the greatest joys bring challenge. And children with special needs inspire a very, very special love. To the families of special-needs... [APPLAUSE] To the families of special-needs children all across this country, I have a message for you: For years, you've sought to make America a more welcoming place for your sons and daughters. And I pledge to you that, if we're elected, you will have a friend and advocate in the White House. [APPLAUSE] | Palin can identify personally with parents of children with disabilities and mental illnesses. |

| | |
|---|---|
| And Todd is a story all by himself. He's a lifelong commercial fisherman and a production operator in the oil fields of Alaska's North Slope, and a proud member of the United Steelworkers Union. And Todd is a world champion snow machine racer. [APPLAUSE] | Palin's husband Todd's background is used to appeal to blue-collar voters. |

CHARACTER

**185**

(*cont.*)

**Sarah Palin's use of *ethos* in her 2008 Republican Convention Speech (*cont.*)**

| | |
|---|---|
| Throw in his Yup'ik Eskimo ancestry, and it all makes for quite a package. | |
| And we met in high school. And two decades and five children later, he's still my guy. | *Pathos* – the long-term college romance helps soften her image. |
| My mom and dad both worked at the elementary school in our small town. And among the many things I owe them is a simple lesson that I've learned, that this is America, and every woman can walk through every door of opportunity. And my parents are here tonight. [APPLAUSE] | Parents are employed to evoke the virtues of old-fashioned education and small-town values. |
| I signed up for the PTA because I wanted to make my kids' public education even better. And when I ran for city council, I didn't need focus groups and voter profiles because I knew those voters, and I knew their families, too.<br>Before I became governor of the great state of Alaska... [APPLAUSE]... I was mayor of my hometown. And since our opponents in this presidential election seem to look down on that experience, let me explain to them what the job involved. [APPLAUSE]<br>I guess – I guess a small-town mayor is sort of like a community organiser, except that you have actual responsibilities. [APPLAUSE] | Palin evokes her journey to show she's not a typical professional politician – unlike Obama (using *antithesis*, *irony*, and *praeteritio*). |
| I'm not a member of the permanent political establishment. And... [APPLAUSE] I've learned quickly these last few days that, if you're not a member in good standing of the Washington elite, then some in | Palin identifies herself with the values and character of authentic politicians, not the liberal establishment. |

the media consider a candidate
unqualified for that reason alone.
[AUDIENCE BOOS]
But here's a little newsflash for those
reporters and commentators: I'm
not going to Washington to seek
their good opinion. I'm going to
Washington to serve the people of
this great country. [APPLAUSE]

In many ways, Palin's convention speech was *all* about *ethos*. It demonstrates how, in recent decades, the Republicans have managed to raise the discussion of character to an art form. It certainly worked with this handpicked loyalist audience, as the constant applause and chants demonstrated. But in milder form perhaps, Palin appeared to suffer from the same problem as Teddy Kennedy: the disconnect between the old-fashioned small-town Christian values she professed in her speeches, and the reality of her own life as a career woman whose own family failed quite spectacularly to live up to those values. Defiant or not, it seems the voters valued the two things she couldn't project: experience and gravitas. Or as they put it in Rome:

> *satis eloquentiae, sapientiae parum*
> plenty of eloquence, too little wisdom.

Cicero, as we have seen, defined the ideal orator and statesman as someone able to combine oratorical flair with depth of character and substance. Palin had the first, but many judged Obama to have all three. In the next chapter we look at this third quality – substance – and how to project it effectively in speech.

CHARACTER

# Chapter 7
# **Evidence**

**1**

From the preceding chapters, one might assume that by employing style, projecting character and appealing to emotion, the gifted orator or speechwriter could produce a great speech by saying anything or nothing. It's true that technique alone can produce wittiness. Take the cheeky speech made by the sixteen-year-old William Hague to the British Conservative Party conference in Blackpool in 1977:

> There is at least one school, I think it is in London, where the pupils are allowed to win just one race each, for fear that to win more would make the other pupils seem inferior. That is a classic illustration of the socialist state which draws nearer with every Labour government and which conservatives have never reversed. It's all right for some of you [WAVING TOWARDS THE AUDIENCE AND MRS THATCHER]; half of you won't be here in 30 or 40 years' time! [LAUGHTER, APPLAUSE]

It thrilled the audience, including Mrs Thatcher, and set Hague up for a lifetime of invitations and income from the professional speaking circuit. His speaking abilities also helped him become the leader of the Tory party. It's also an excellent example of how to use humour to connect with the forum. But great? No.

As Aristotle recognised, the character of the speaker and the emotional disposition of the audience provided only part of the speech's proof. A third set of qualities was required; qualities inherent to the speech itself: purpose, substance, structure, evidence, logic; or what the Greeks called *logos*.

## 2

———————————— 🐾 🐾 🐾 ————————————

Appealing to the emotions of the audience takes courage and skill, and getting it wrong can leave the speaker looking foolish. Afraid, many compensate by taking refuge in argument and evidence – lots of it. What they don't do is present this meaty and ultimately most important part of the speech in an appealing form. This is in many ways the hardest of the speechwriter's tasks, and the one usually given the least thought.

So where do we start?

The Greeks and Romans give us a clue. Let's look again at what they called the divisions of speech:

1 **prologue**: the opening remarks that grab the audience's attention and sympathies
2 **narrative**: the speaker's major contention or case
3 **proofs**: the arguments used to support the speaker's contention or case
4 **refutation**: refuting the arguments of the opposing case
5 **conclusion**: summing up or ending by cinching the case or ramming the major points home.

Points 1 and 5 are chiefly concerned with character and emotion to win the audience's trust and close the deal with them. Our concern here is with points 3 to 5, where the three substantial tasks of the speechwriter reside: to state the speech's purpose, prove it, and destroy the opposing case.

Before taking on these three duties, something else must be clarified: the objective. What is the speech's aim? To entertain or impress? To prosecute a case or uncover a truth about the past? To talk about the future and make a claim for leadership? Hence the classifications of speech:

1  **display**: a speech in praise of others, such as a eulogy, or a formal occasion for showing off the speaker's eloquence
2  **forensic**: a legal speech in a law court, concerned about past events
3  **deliberative**: a political speech in an executive council, legislature or public assembly, primarily about the future.

This may seem obvious, but speechmakers sometimes gets this basic starting point wrong – by showing off with no substance, which makes them look lightweight; prosecuting when they should be inspiring, which makes them look negative; or discussing principles when they should be making a case, which proves they haven't got a case to make.

# 3
— 🎵🎵🎵 —

Let's begin with narrative. Every great speech needs a purpose, and the greatest speeches state their purpose clearly and succinctly upfront.

It sometimes takes courage and a willingness to confront an audience with an unpleasant message. A fine example is the speech by Edward R. Murrow, played by David Strathairn, which opens and closes the 2005 movie *Good Night, and Good Luck*, directed by George Clooney.

The script involves a dramatic reworking of an actual speech Murrow made to the Radio-Television News Directors Association in Chicago on 15 October 1958. Murrow, who had reported the Battle of Britain to American radio audiences in 1940 (experiencing first-hand the impact of Churchill's oratory), flown on bombing raids over Europe, and reported the liberation of the concentration camp at Buchenwald, understood what people had died for in that war, and he was determined that the survivors made that sacrifice worthwhile. He had also studied oratory at university. His theme was the need to ensure that television is more than just 'wires and lights in a box' designed to entertain us, but something that can inform, enlighten and play a part in the protection of our democratic freedoms – not something a television industry audience in 1958 (or at any time) would necessarily have wanted to hear:

> This might just do nobody any good. At the end of this discourse a few people may accuse this reporter of fouling his own comfortable nest, and your organisation may be accused of having given hospitality to heretical and even dangerous ideas. But the elaborate structure of networks, advertising agencies, and sponsors will not be shaken or altered.

> It is my desire, if not my duty, to try to talk to you journeymen with some candour about what is happening to radio and television. And if what I say is responsible, I, alone, am responsible for the saying of it.

> Our history will be what we make it. And if there are any historians about 50 or 100 years from now – and there should be preserved the kinescopes of one week of all three networks – they will there find, recorded in black and white and in colour, evidence of decadence, escapism, and insulation from the realities of the world in which we live. We are currently wealthy, fat, comfortable, and complacent. We have a built-in allergy to unpleasant or disturbing information.

> Our mass media reflect this.

But unless we get up off our fat surpluses and recognise that television in the main is being used to distract, delude, amuse, and insulate us, then television, and those who finance it, those who look at it, and those who work at it, may see a totally different picture too late.

It's a call to a life of seriousness. Murrow's speech illustrates how having a purpose in a speech is also connected to *ethos*, because saying something unwelcome or challenging involves courage and character. We've seen in chapter 6 how John F. Kennedy used the announcement of the Apollo program to argue that part of its point was to stretch our intelligence and ingenuity and bring out humanity's best qualities. What's also notable about that speech is the clarity with which it expresses its purpose:

> I believe that this nation should commit itself to achieving the goal, before this decade is out, of landing a man on the Moon and returning him safely to the Earth. No single space project in this period will be more impressive to mankind or more important for the long-range exploration of space; and none will be so difficult or expensive to accomplish.

Unremarkable in some ways, but it has a wonderfully simple elegance, concreteness and directness. There is no hedging about timeframes, no maybes, no jargon, no using the difficulties involved in the enterprise as an escape clause – Kennedy actually highlights the difficulties to show his determination to overcome them. Even the word 'commit'– which in recent years has become a euphemism for lack of commitment and a hedge against unforeseen circumstances ('We are committed to going to the Moon, unless of course . . .') – is used in its proper manner, which is to imply that we *will* do it.

Imagine if he'd said this, which will sound all too familiar to those suffering under the rule of technocrats:

> Our preferred outcome would be that, within a reasonable timeframe, taking into account all the variables that can

affect a mission of such complicated dimensions – including human frailty, technological malfunctions and plain bad luck – to plan and execute successfully, using all the expertise at our disposal, a staffed mission to that luminous satellite that orbits our planet, the moon, and – God willing and with good fortune – bring the astronauts back in one piece. But safety for all involved will, of course, will be our prime concern, which won't be compromised for any reason.

Even though John F. Kennedy never lived to see it, before the decade was out the USA indeed did land a man on the Moon and return him safely to Earth. That achievement involved a lot more than words, but by conveying purpose and (genuine) commitment, words can instil belief and direct human effort. There's no finer example than in Churchill's 'blood, toil, tears and sweat' address to the House of Commons upon becoming prime minister, first discussed in chapter 3. Its purpose was clear: to signal he wants Britain to fight on until victory. Note its use of *anthypophora* to answer what the policy and aim of his new government is, and its use of *anaphora* to emphasise that without victory there is no survival:

We have before us an ordeal of the most grievous kind. We have before us many, many long months of struggle and of suffering. You ask, what is our policy? I can say: It is to wage war, by sea, land and air, with all our might and with all the strength that God can give us; to wage war against a monstrous tyranny, never surpassed in the dark, lamentable catalogue of human crime. That is our policy. You ask, what is our aim? I can answer in one word: It is victory, victory at all costs, victory in spite of all terror, victory, however long and hard the road may be; for without victory, there is no survival. Let that be realised; no survival for the British Empire, no survival for all that the British Empire has stood for, no survival for the urge and impulse of the ages, that mankind will move forward towards its goal. But I take up my task with buoyancy and hope. I feel sure that our cause will not be suffered to fail among men. At this time I feel entitled to claim the aid of all, and I say, 'Come then, let us go forward together with our united strength'.

Churchill left us in no doubt about what the goal was and what the cost of failure would be. And victory was achieved; monstrous tyranny was defeated. Again, it took more than words, but without the resolve, expressed through words, the result would have been surrender.

# 4

On stating one's purpose, the task of the speechwriter is to make a case for it.

This is where it is easy to run into difficulties, because great issues – while morally often right and wrong – usually involve complexities that can't be dismissed easily or simplified without making the speaker seem shallow and flippant, and without insulting the intelligence of the audience.

In such situations the role of the speechwriter is to make the complex simple, but without simplifying in the sense of dumbing it down. As a good lawyer does, the aim is to make the crucial points absolutely clear.

In chapter 2 we saw how Robert Harris handled Cicero's denunciation of Catilina in his second Cicero novel, *Lustrum*. Harris, a former political editor of *The Observer*, knows his politics, and here he is again, portraying Cicero zeroing in on what's really the issue behind a complex and intentionally opaque piece of legislation proposed by his enemies:

'Now you all know that this morning, before the sun had even risen, the bill of the tribune Servilius Rullus, for which we have been waiting so long, was finally posted in the forum . . . Here is the bill, and I earnestly assure you that I have examined it as carefully as is possible in the circumstances of today and the time allowed me, and I have reached a firm opinion . . . It is nothing less,' he said, 'than a dagger, pointed towards the body politic, that we are being invited to plunge into our own heart! . . . A dagger' he repeated, 'with a long blade.' He licked his thumb and flicked open the first notebook. 'Clause one, page one, line one. The election of the ten commissioners . . . '

In this way he cut straight through the posturing and sentiment to the nub of the issue, which was, as it always is, power. 'Who proposes the commission?' he asked. 'Rullus Who determines who is to elect the commissioners? Rullus . . . ' The patrician senators began joining in, chanting the unfortunate tribune's name after every question. 'Who declares the results?'

'Rullus,' boomed the senate.

'Who alone is guaranteed a place as a commissioner?'

'Rullus!'

'Who wrote the bill?'

'Rullus!' And the house collapsed in tears of laughter. [The bill had, as everyone knew, been written by Caesar and Crassus.]

Harris' neat fictional speech alerts us to another secret of using evidence: it doesn't need to be separated from the *tropes, schemes, ethos* and *pathos* that bring the rest of a speech to life.

It may be objected that this is fine in the Roman Senate (especially a fictional one), but it takes an extraordinary kind of rhetorical genius and political courage to make a detailed and serious speech in the world of today, with its media spin and three-minute attention span. This is true. But it can be done.

Race is a particularly difficult issue for any politician to discuss at length. Getting people to acknowledge their bigotry and face up to unwelcome facts is hard – far more difficult than dog whistling – as we examine elsewhere in this book in speeches by Enoch Powell and the Australians John Howard and Pauline Hanson. Too often, the realistic politician allows bigotries to remain un-confronted. Sometimes, though, someone speaks up, and history always applauds.

A perfect example of this is one of the most controversial, arguably most politically costly, but certainly most important speeches in Australian history. In June 1992 in the Mabo case, the High Court of Australia handed down a major decision that rejected the fiction that Australia was, for practical purposes, uninhabited and unowned before European settlement – a difficult concept for many non-Indigenous Australians to stomach. The case had major implications for property law and Indigenous policy, forcing the parliament to re-examine both, and came on top of other official revelations about the treatment of Australia's Indigenous peoples.

Pressure built, and on 10 December 1992 Prime Minister Paul Keating used the launch of the Year of the World's Indigenous People to address the issue. Written by Don Watson (and, importantly, unseen by anyone else in the Prime Minister's office apart from the Prime Minister himself), the speech caused a sensation. Watson, perhaps modestly, perhaps in deference to Keating's limitations with a written text (he was unmatched when it came to *extempore* exchanges, with a devastating facility for withering invective) wrote afterwards that 'Comparisons with Martin Luther King being inevitably invidious, rhetorical fireworks and high sentiment were not attempted'.

This was true, but that doesn't mean the speech was prosaic, because, as the following extract reveals, intentionally or not, it was a model of Ciceronean *middle style* eloquence. The reader by now will recognise a number of devices, including *epanalepsis*, *anaphora*, *epiphora*, *erotema* and *pathos*. Its genius lies in making such techniques seem unforced and natural. In this it is consistent with the particular style of Watson – not *stentorian* like Sorensen (loudly sounding a call to duty and sacrifice), but with a pastoral, suburban sense of *ethos* (if you want to know what sacrifice is, Watson says in other famous speeches, just look around). Most of all, the speech is notable for the way it presents an unpopular argument and supports it with evidence – a calm statement of facts that the majority of Australians didn't want to hear, or, because the facts were largely taboo, had never been able to hear:

> The starting point might be to recognise that the problem starts with us non-Aboriginal Australians. It begins, I think, with the act of recognition. Recognition that it was we who did the dispossessing. [AUDIENCE STOPS CATCALLING] We took the traditional lands and smashed the traditional way of life. We brought the disasters. The alcohol. We committed the murders. We took the children from their mothers. [APPLAUSE] We practised discrimination and exclusion. It was our ignorance and our prejudice. And our failure to imagine these things being done to us. With some noble exceptions, we failed to make the most basic human response and enter into their hearts and minds. We failed to ask, 'How would I feel if this were done to me?' As a consequence, we failed to see that what we were doing degraded all of us.

As with the Gettysburg Address, that speech showed how, by restating the official view of history, a speech can alter the meaning of a constitution. It had its partner sixteen years later when the new Labor Prime Minister, Kevin Rudd, made another landmark speech to officially apologise to the Stolen Generations – the Aboriginal and Torres Strait Islander peoples whose children's forcible removal from their families was official government policy from 1909 to 1969.

Barack Obama similarly asked Americans to confront their racial politics during the primary campaign of 2008. Obama had consciously set out not to make race the central issue of his election, but when his former family pastor, the radical African-American preacher the Reverend Jeremiah Wright, was captured on film making controversial and 'unpatriotic' comments about the racist nature of American society, Obama was forced to bring forward a planned speech on the race issue. Courageously, for someone in his position, who could have been excused for focus testing a mealy-mouthed response to distance himself from Wright, Obama asked the audience to examine the past and understand why Wright and people like him thought the way they did, why Wright's views were mirrored in those of white Americans, and why they both, together, needed to grasp that moment in history to overcome the stalemate. This, he argued, was a starting point for solving the problems all Americans had in common, such as the lack of rights to universal health insurance. It was a complex argument to make in an election campaign; certainly few others would have had the courage to try it.

Known as the 'Towards a more perfect union' speech, given on 18 March 2008 in Philadelphia, like Keating's speech it is noticeable for its willingness to confront the unpleasant facts of history, and in doing so provides an important narrative that makes Obama's case:

> As William Faulkner once wrote, 'The past isn't dead and buried. In fact, it isn't even past.' We do not need to recite here the history of racial injustice in this country. But we do need to remind ourselves that so many of the disparities that exist in the African-American community today can be directly traced to inequalities passed on from an earlier generation that suffered under the brutal legacy of slavery and Jim Crow.
>
> Segregated schools were, and are, inferior schools; we still haven't fixed them, fifty years after *Brown v. Board of Education*, and the inferior education they provided, then and now, helps explain the pervasive achievement gap between today's black and white students.
>
> Legalised discrimination – where blacks were prevented, often through violence, from owning property, or loans were not granted to African-American business owners, or black homeowners could not access FHA mortgages, or blacks were excluded from unions, or the police force, or

fire departments – meant that black families could not amass any meaningful wealth to bequeath to future generations. That history helps explain the wealth and income gap between black and white, and the concentrated pockets of poverty that persists in so many of today's urban and rural communities.

A lack of economic opportunity among black men, and the shame and frustration that came from not being able to provide for one's family, contributed to the erosion of black families – a problem that welfare policies for many years may have worsened. And the lack of basic services in so many urban black neighbourhoods – parks for kids to play in, police walking the beat, regular garbage pick-up and building code enforcement – all helped create a cycle of violence, blight and neglect that continue to haunt us.

This is the reality in which Reverend Wright and other African-Americans of his generation grew up. They came of age in the late fifties and early sixties, a time when segregation was still the law of the land and opportunity was systematically constricted. What's remarkable is not how many failed in the face of discrimination, but rather how many men and women overcame the odds; how many were able to make a way out of no way for those like me who would come after them.

But for all those who scratched and clawed their way to get a piece of the American Dream, there were many who didn't make it – those who were ultimately defeated, in one way or another, by discrimination. That legacy of defeat was passed on to future generations – those young men and increasingly young women who we see standing on street corners or languishing in our prisons, without hope or prospects for the future. Even for those blacks who did make it, questions of race, and racism, continue to define their worldview in fundamental ways. For the men and

women of Reverend Wright's generation, the memories of
humiliation and doubt and fear have not gone away . . .

In the lead up to the speech, Obama's chief adviser David Axelrod
had told him what was at stake. 'Do you guys understand, this could
be it. This could be the whole campaign.' Such was the nervousness
about going 'off-message' on race. But, receiving the final draft by
email from his candidate on the morning of the event, Axelrod
responded stating: 'This is why you should be president'.

It is worth noting that 'Towards a more perfect union' never
prevented the American people from taking the biggest step imaginable in moving beyond the racial stalemate – electing an African-
American as their president. Perhaps Obama was right, and a speech
had made a small but important contribution to allowing America
to move on from the racial stalemate that had held back social
reform for so long.

# 5

---

The Redfern Park and 'Towards a more perfect union' speeches
were organised around important and highly complex arguments
about empathy and history. Facts made their cases, but, interestingly, there wasn't a single statistic in sight. This is curious, and
important. It alerts us to something too often forgotten today: facts
do not begin and end with statistics, or modelling, or long quo-
tations from earnest academic papers. In fact, used unwisely and
excessively, facts in the form of statistics and superfluous details
can destroy a speech.

Which brings us to the subject so often mangled in
speech – economics. Economic speeches too often use statistics
poorly. The bored non-economist will know the agony of sitting
through speeches that seem to have been written by actuaries –
full of long lists of statistics and projections loosely connected by
a theory so complex you need an economics degree *summa cum*

*laude* to understand it. This may be acceptable at a luncheon for the society of economists, and it may occasionally be necessary to make a technical case for, say, the efficiency and equity of a new tax on mining companies (in such cases it's necessary to project your technical command of the subject matter even to non-specialist listeners), but not for a public address. It forgets something: economics is about people, not numbers. The best economics speeches take this as their starting point.

Let's look once more at Barack Obama; in this case at the way he talks about economics. Obama was elected during the greatest economic crash since the Great Depression. Known more as a social policy thinker, did he have what it took to face down the crisis in the way that Franklin D. Roosevelt did in his first inaugural address (discussed in chapter 4)? The answer, rhetorically at least, is yes. The pressure was certainly on in his first State of the Union Address on 22 February 2009, where tried to re-inject confidence back into an economy plunging into recession, repossession and retrenchment.

> I know that for many Americans watching right now, the state of our economy is a concern that rises above all others. And rightly so. If you haven't been personally affected by this recession, you probably know someone who has – a friend; a neighbour; a member of your family. You don't need to hear another list of statistics to know that our economy is in crisis, because you live it every day. It's the worry you wake up with and the source of sleepless nights. It's the job you thought you'd retire from but now have lost; the business you built your dreams upon that's now hanging by a thread; the college acceptance letter your child had to put back in the envelope. The impact of this recession is real, and it is everywhere.
>
> But while our economy may be weakened and our confidence shaken; though we are living through difficult

and uncertain times, tonight I want every American to know this: we will rebuild, we will recover, and the United States of America will emerge stronger than before.

The weight of this crisis will not determine the destiny of this nation. The answers to our problems don't lie beyond
• our reach. They exist in our laboratories and universities; in our fields and our factories; in the imaginations of our entrepreneurs and the pride of the hardest-working people on Earth. Those qualities that have made America the greatest force of progress and prosperity in human history we still possess in ample measure. What is required now is for this country to pull together, confront boldly the challenges we face, and take responsibility for our future once more.

There are no statistics. There is no need. As Obama points out, everyone can see, almost feel, for themselves the nature and scale of what is happening. Note also the sense of purpose conveyed ('What is required now is . . . ').

This isn't to say that statistics, when providing genuine news and information, cannot be powerful – although it must be remembered that many statistics have little credibility and therefore constitute weak evidence. Fresh facts, even old facts presented in a surprising new way, can have an explosive impact.

One of the best examples of this is a speech all about the revelation of facts – Nikita Khrushchev's secret speech to the Soviet Communist Party's 20th Party Congress on 25 February 1956, in which he denounced the cult of Stalin, the tyrant's wartime incompetence and the crimes against freedom he had committed. In some ways what Khrushchev revealed wasn't news at all, because the people listening would have witnessed the cult of the individual, the wartime failings and the mass arrests and executions first-hand. Every listener would have had a relative killed or taken prisoner in the military disasters of the early months of 1941, or a friend arrested after the 17th Party Congress of 1934, and many would have conveyed Stalin's orders or have done the arresting and torturing themselves. Perhaps what was important was that these facts, provided for the first time by the leader of the Communist Party himself, were being released at all. The release of the facts could mean only one thing: a political thaw was underway. They were a bombshell. It was possible once again to speak openly in public about things everyone knew. Here are the real facts given by Khrushchev, monstrous in their proportions:

> Of the 139 members and candidates of the central committee who were elected at the 17th congress, 98 persons, 70 per cent, were arrested and shot. It is inconceivable that a congress so composed could have elected a central committee in which a majority would prove to be enemies of the party. Delegates were active participants in the building of our socialist state; many of them suffered and fought during the pre-revolutionary years; they fought their enemies valiantly and often nervelessly looked into the face of death. How, then, can we believe that such people had joined the camps of the enemies of socialism? This was the result of the abuse of power by Stalin. On the evening of December 1 1934 on Stalin's initiative, the secretary of the presidium signed the following directive: '1. Investigative agencies are directed to speed up the cases of those accused of acts of terror; 2. Judicial organs are directed not to hold up execution in order to consider pardon; 3. The organs of the commissariat of internal affairs are directed to execute the death sentences immediately after the passage of sentences.' This directive became the basis for mass acts of abuse. The accused were deprived of any possibility that their cases might be re-examined, even when they stated before the court that their 'confessions' were secured by force.

A well-researched and well-chosen fact can help other types of proof in your speeches, including character and emotion. As we've seen elsewhere, one of the most important types of oratory is the military memorial speech. Sometimes what prevents them from becoming boilerplate and makes their emotional appeal work are facts. There are few things more able to invoke rage or pity than the unmediated realities of war. Faced with the need to produce an important ANZAC Day address to a Washington DC audience for the Australian Treasurer Wayne Swan, I found the answer in the National Archives in the form of Swan's grandfather's service records. Nothing could encapsulate the Australian Great War story better than what happened to Private 1984 David Temple Swan. A labourer who enlisted at thirty-seven in search of glory, he was gassed and wounded by shellfire at the battle of Messines, invalided out of the frontline with shell shock and strain after the battles to stop the German Spring Offensive of 1918, and died relatively young of war-related illness after struggling to farm the citizen-soldier block given to him by a grateful nation. The facts tell the story of adventure, reality and tragic consequence. They need no elaboration:

> For an Australian the proudest boast is that your ancestors fought with General Sir John Monash . . . My own grandfather was such a man.

## 6

The question arises: How should facts be chosen to have the maximum impact in a speech? There are three rules – all of which I learnt myself editing the drafts sent up to government ministers' offices by junior departmental speechwriters:

- **Rule number one**: making a list of programs or statistics longer and more comprehensive does not make it more interesting or more persuasive.
- **Rule number two**: making a list of programs or statistics longer and more comprehensive does not make it more interesting or more persuasive.

- **Rule number three**: making a list of programs or statistics longer and more comprehensive does not make it more interesting or more persuasive.

As you now know after reading rules 1–3, reciting long lists to an audience that has come along to hear you, hoping to be enlightened and entertained, slows down the pulse of a speech and often forfeits the audience's attention (even if expressed with *tricolon, repetition* and *sarcasm*).

The answer is to ask yourself a question: what is the *killer fact* that makes my case? If you're working for a government and you don't have a killer fact, commission someone to discover it, because it is what clinches a speech's case after the audience has been made receptive by the other devices we have discussed. One crunching blow has far more impact that one thousand light slaps. Like a boxer, when using facts, get in quick, land your hardest punch, get out.

That's what Al Gore does in *An Inconvenient Truth*. As we have remarked before, it's the movie of a highly sophisticated stump speech. In addition to projecting character, as we saw in chapter 6, the speech presents facts extremely effectively – something even those who disagree with the science will admit to their annoyance. Complicated scientific explanations that would otherwise lose the audience are provided through entertaining means, such as cartoons. And the killer facts hit home. This is done in two ways – by using single and multiple facts.

Think of Gore's main killer fact. At the crucial point of his address he plots on the screen behind him 650 000 years of changes in the concentration of $CO_2$ in the atmosphere against 650 000 years of changes in world temperatures to demonstrate a correlation. Then he uses the device of a cherry picker to take him up the wall to the point where $CO_2$ concentrations are now, and then up further to where they will be in less than 50 years from now. (This can be thought of as a visual form of the technique of *hyperbole*.) His point is obvious: $CO_2$ and temperature rises will be off the chart and the world is headed for catastrophe – unless we do something about it . . . He uses the technique again with other killer facts, such as the speedy projection of photographs of the world's retreating glaciers. The inference: there will soon be few or none of these beautiful natural phenomena left. Presenting multiple pieces of evidence, even statistics, works well when done staccato fashion like this. The crucial point is not to get bogged down and introduce facts of declining force simply for the sake of using them.

Aristotle called this type of argument *inductive reasoning* – making inferences based upon observed patterns, or simple repetition. Gore illustrates it perfectly.

For an example of *deductive reasoning* – which attempts to show that a conclusion necessarily follows from a set of premises – we need go no further than one of the memorable lines of Martin Luther King's 'I have a dream' speech:

> We hold these truths to be self-evident; that all men are
> created equal.

All else in the speech follows from this famous *allusion* to the second sentence of the *Declaration of Independence* and the Gettysburg Address – freedom, equality, the end of segregation everywhere.

Having made these points about the need to be careful in the choice of facts in a speech, there may be times when you need to use multiple pieces of evidence in an attempt to overwhelm your opponent by sheer weight of evidence. The technique is similar to the effect of an elephant leaning on a house – it may take time, but the house will eventually collapse. In these circumstances the emphasis must always be on dramatic presentation in such a way as to emphasise the increasing pressure and the imminence of a cave in.

Perhaps the most famous recent case of this type of use of multiple examples of evidence is US Secretary of State Colin Powell's presentation to the UN Security Council on 5 February 2003 to make the case that Iraq had breeched the conditions of Resolution 1441, clearing the way for UN-sanctioned military action. The speech, according to Powell at the time, listed 'an accumulation of facts and disturbing patterns of behaviour' proving that Iraq was manufacturing weapons of mass destruction, persecuting minorities and had links to the Al Qaeda terrorist network. Lasting 76 minutes, the speech drew evidence from taped conversations, satellite photography, human intelligence sources, testimony of Iraqi defectors, and the findings of the UN's own weapons inspectors. Sadly for Powell's reputation, many of the facts in the speech were subsequently exposed as faked, exaggerated or plain wishful thinking on the part of the US administration. The inclusion of many of the pieces of evidence had been the subject of ferocious debate. Powell admitted publicly that the speech was a blot on his record. Although it never convinced the UN to endorse the invasion that followed, the speech succeeded in its short-term aim, which was to build a (seemingly) weighty case for war that appeared overwhelming to those whose opinions counted – the US public, the British Government and media agencies around the world that were backing the war. It was morally dubious, but it worked – and the moral implications of this sort of dishonest speechmaking are discussed in chapter 8.

# 7

ℝ ℝ ℝ

The final *logos*-related job of a speech is *refutation* – the undermining or knocking out of opposing arguments. A killer fact or revelation can do it like a good right hook to the jaw.

To illustrate this we can look to another famous, far happier, address to the UN Security Council – by US Ambassador Adlai Stevenson. Stevenson was a noted liberal congressman, whose brilliant oratory made him, like Kennedy, a darling of the Democratic Party rank and file, but who was twice defeated for the presidency. On 25 October 1962, at the height of the Cuban Missile Crisis, in an emergency session of the Security Council, Stevenson asked the Soviet ambassador for a 'yes' or 'no' answer as to whether the Soviets were installing nuclear missiles on Cuban soil. Waiting,

Stevenson interjected, 'I am prepared to wait for my answer until hell freezes over.' Then, dramatically, after the Soviets implied they hadn't installed missiles, Stevenson delivered the *coup de grâce* in the form of photographs proving irrefutably that in fact the Soviets had installed such missiles. This time the evidence was real.

The Soviets were forced to back off; war was averted; and – perhaps to illustrate neatly Cicero's belief that the hope of the world lies in the hands of statesmen who can combine moral uprightness, depth of character, breadth of knowledge and oratorical ability – John F. Kennedy, advised by men like his speechwriter Ted Sorensen and his brother Bobby, deftly brought the world back from the brink of nuclear annihilation. As Kennedy himself had said, 'in the long history of the world, only a few generations have been granted the role of defending freedom in its hour of maximum danger'. His generation passed that test, and in doing so proved that great rhetoric, great substance, great style and great *logos* made a great statesman.

# Chapter 8
# Morality

## 1

───────────── ༭ ༭ ༭ ─────────────

Now, armed with an understanding of forum, style, *ethos*, *pathos* and *logos*, the speechwriter confronts morality and the question: should the arts of oratory really be used at all?

## 2

───────────── ༭ ༭ ༭ ─────────────

The question of whether oratory is a force for good or evil has been debated since the birth of trained oratory itself.

In 423 BC, only 4 years after Gorgias brought the craze of stylised speechmaking to Athens, the playwright Aristophanes memorably satirised its exponents.

His play *Clouds* opens with Strepsiades taking his loose-spending playboy son Pheidippides for a walk through Athens, with the intention of telling him it's time to settle down, give up gambling and horse-racing and repay his debts. Father's well-chosen route takes them past the headquarters of the sophists.

| | |
|---|---|
| STREPSIADES: | Look over this way. You see that nice little door and that nice little house? |
| PHEIDIPPIDES: | Yes. What is it, actually, father? |
| STREPSIADES: | It is a Thinkery for intellectual souls . . . And if you pay them well, they can teach you how to win a case whether you're in the right or not. |
| PHEIDIPPIDES: | Who are these people? |
| STREPSIADES: | I don't quite remember their name. They're very fine reflective intellectuals. |
| PHEIDIPPIDES: | Yecch! I know the villains. You mean those pale-faced bare-footed quacks such as that wretched Socrates and Chaerephon . . . |
| STREPSIADES: | [*desperately*]: My most beloved son – I beg of you – do go and study with them! |
| PHEIDIPPIDES: | What do you want me to learn? |
| STREPSIADES: | They say they have two Arguments in there – Right and Wrong they call them – and one of them, Wrong, can always win its case even when justice is against it. Well, if you can learn this Wrongful Argument, then of all these debts I've run into because of you, I needn't pay anyone an obol of them ever. |

Strepsiades wants his son to grow up – and start making money! And he's heard around town that if you want to get ahead in the world, the sophists are the ones to talk to. They don't waste time with the disinterested search for truth or with the traditions that uphold the accepted order but teach their clients how to gain advantage.

By making 'the weaker argument defeat the stronger' (as Plato's Socrates put it in his defence trial) they supposedly helped the ambitious talk their way into power and fortune.

To the conservative Aristophanes the rhetorical training offered by the sophists was anathema, likely to lead to the triumph of good over bad and the subversion of the natural order as upstarts learnt how to manipulate the political system to their own advantage. The end result could only be the triumph of the very worst aspect of democracy: anarchic populism.

As we saw in chapter 2, Socrates was no sophist – in fact the very opposite, although in a different way his teaching could work to undermine established authority. (And the story goes that he attended the first performance of *The Clouds* and stood up to acknowledge the audience.) But by defending his mentor Socrates against the charge of sophism Plato kicked off a debate about the ethical superiority of pure philosophy over rhetoric that became one of the most celebrated academic arguments of all time, which is still being played out today.

# 3

The basic question is this: by revealing how to sway audiences of the unlearned, have the teachers of political oratory given evil people the means to do harm? Plato certainly believed so. Two thousand years later one example in particular suggests he had a point: Adolf Hitler.

Here's how one of the foremost historians of Nazi Germany describes Hitler's oratory:

> While conventional right-wing politicians delivered lectures, or spoke in a style that was orotund and pompous, flat and dull, or rough and brutish, Hitler followed the model of Social-Democratic orators such as [Kurt] Eisner, or the left-wing agitators from whom he later claimed to have learned in Vienna. And he gained much of his oratorical success by telling his audiences what they wanted to hear. He used simple, straightforward language that ordinary people could understand, short sentences, powerful,

emotive slogans. Often beginning a speech quietly, to capture his audience's attention, he would gradually build to a climax, his deep, rather hoarse voice would rise in pitch, climbing in crescendo to a ranting and screaming finale, accompanied by carefully rehearsed dramatic gestures, his face glistening with sweat, his lank dark hair falling forward over his face as he worked his audience into a frenzy of emotion. There were no qualifications in what he said; everything was absolute, uncompromising, irrevocable, undeviating, unalterable, final. He seemed, as many who listened to his early speeches testified, to speak straight from the heart, and to express their own deepest fears and desires. Increasingly too, he exuded self-confidence, belief in the ultimate triumph of his party, even a sense of destiny. His speeches often began with an account of his own poverty-stricken early life, to which he drew an implicit parallel with the downcast, downtrodden and desperate state of Germany after the First World War, then, his voice rising, he would describe his own political awakening, and point to its counterpart in Germany's future recovery and return to glory. Without necessarily using overtly religious language, Hitler appealed to religious archetypes of suffering, humiliation, redemption and resurrection lodged deep within his listeners' psyche...

Style, *pathos*, *ethos*, forum and delivery, but not *logos*!

It was Hitler's mesmeric oratory that propelled him to leadership of the German far right. His ability to attract huge crowds to his rallies made him indispensible to the Nazi Party, enabling him to dominate it with his ideas. One Nazi said that after hearing Hitler speak in person, 'there was only one thing for me, either to win with Adolf Hitler or die with him'. Millions felt the same. Watching the old newsreel footage today, one can see how this happened.

Oratory on its own did not bring Hitler to power. With-out an audience made hungry for hate by defeat, unemployment

Hitler practises his mesmeric craft. Photo: © Getty Images.

and hyperinflation, Hitler would have come to nothing. But stripped of his oratory he would most likely have been just another run-of-the-mill beer-hall and street-corner anti-Semite. He would have come to little, and the Holocaust would have been far less likely.

Demagogues still plague us. In the late 1990s Australia found itself in the grip of one such person – the xenophobic populist Pauline Hanson.

Hanson's maiden speech to the House of Representatives in 1996, written for her by her onetime adviser John Pasquarelli, is possibly the most nation-changing Australian political speech of modern times – giving politicians the licence to once again talk openly about race – and is a polished example of classical rhetoric.

It has all the techniques of the speechwriter's craft, like this *pathos* and *ethos*, which had the demos nodding in agreement:

> I come here not as a polished politician but as a woman who has had her fair share of life's knocks.

> I may be only 'a fish-and-chip shop lady', but some of these economists need to get their heads out of the textbooks and get a job in the real world. I would not even let one of them handle my grocery shopping.

Note how, like Mark Antony, she denies being polished. Her words have some nice *anaphora* and parallel construction that would be the envy of a Sorensen or a Noonan – although there are some nasty echoes (try replacing 'flag' with 'leader' and then translating it into German):

> To survive in peace and harmony, united and strong, we must have one people, one nation, one flag . . .

> if I can invite whom I want into my home, then I should have a right to a say in who comes into my country.

Even the nervous and unpolished delivery, taken by her supporters as a sign of her genuineness, can be seen as a good example of *syncatabasis* – the art of speaking at the level of your audience, as practised by the Ivy League-educated George W. Bush.

The speaker's subsequent incarceration for electoral fraud and her role as a contestant on the reality television program *Dancing with the Stars* alerts us to the cheapness and dishonest theatricality that typifies this sort of demagoguery. But its success also proves it can be dangerous.

## 4

Given evil orators like Hitler, it's tempting to think Plato was right and that oratory should be banned. Perhaps we could run our political system as we run our courts, where a barrister must stick to the facts and the law or face the wrath of the judge. Indeed, from time to time legislators try to convince us to adopt laws to prevent hate-inciting forms of speech.

But we encounter a serious problem: oratory is an inevitable consequence of a right without which there is no democracy – freedom of speech.

Plato thought he had the answer to the question of how to do away with rhetoric's appeals to the passions over the intellect. But for all his genius, in his book *The Republic* even he could abolish oratory only by presupposing an ideal world ruled by philosopher-kings who alone would possess the right to debate and make decisions for the benefit of all. Plato's classical ideal of rule by educated benign dictators became the twentieth century nightmare of Marx- and Hayek-reading philosopher-autocrats such as Pol Pot and Augusto Pinochet. Experience teaches that where oratory is impossible, murderers, not philosophers, rule. Words are usually replaced by bullets. This is something Plato himself came to realise after his own adventures trying to make philosopher-kings out of the tyrants of Syracuse.

Totalitarian societies have oratory of a kind, but in the absence of the need to persuade (the job of the jackbooted thugs who flank the dictator's rostrum) the speech is replaced by the harangue, logic and facts by hate and lies, and satisfied listeners by cowed onlookers afraid of being the last to start clapping or the first to stop. It comes as no surprise that the only memorable speech to emerge from behind the Iron Curtain (a term Churchill coined in another of his famous speeches) was Nikita Khrushchev's expose of Stalin's cult of the individual; real oratory was only possible once the dictator was dead. The effect on audiences of totalitarian oratory is grasped by George Orwell in *1984* in the scene where it was suddenly announced that Oceania is no longer at war with Eurasia but is at war with Eastasia:

On a scarlet-draped platform an orator of the Inner Party, a small lean man with disproportionately long arms and a large bald skull over which a few lank locks straggled, was haranguing the crowd. A little Rumpelstiltskin figure, contorted with hatred, he gripped the neck of the microphone with one hand while the other, enormous at the end of a bony arm, clawed the air menacingly above his head. His voice, made metallic by the amplifiers, boomed forth an endless catalogue of atrocities, massacres, deportations, lootings, rapings, torture of prisoners, bombing of civilians, lying propaganda, unjust aggressions, broken treaties. It was almost impossible to listen to him without being first convinced and then maddened. At every few moments the fury of the crowd boiled over and the voice of the speaker was drowned by a wild beast-like roaring that rose uncontrollably from thousands of throats. The most savage yells of all came from the schoolchildren. The speech had been proceeding for perhaps twenty minutes when a messenger hurried on to the platform and a scrap of paper was slipped into the speaker's hand. He unrolled and read it without pausing in his speech. Nothing altered in his voice or manner, or in the content of what he was saying, but suddenly the names were different. Without words said, a wave of understanding rippled through the crowd. Oceania was at war with Eastasia! . . . The orator, still gripping the neck of the microphone, his shoulders hunched forward, his free hand clawing at the air, had gone straight on with his speech. One minute more, and the feral roars of rage were again bursting from the crowd. The Hate continued exactly as before, except that the target had been changed.

The thing that impressed Winston in looking back was that the speaker had switched from one line to the other actually in midsentence, not only without a pause, but without even breaking the syntax.

Logic, humour, charm – all the feelings that make humans rise above the animal kingdom – are replaced by hate and fear.

Totalitarian rhetoric – human feelings replaced by hatred and fear. Photo: © Getty Images.

# 5

🦜 🦜 🦜

It's not necessary though to invoke totalitarianism to raise democratic objections to political oratory. Many believe that while speechmaking can't or shouldn't be outlawed, orating – in the sense of employing calculated rhetorical devices – should. This is the journalist's lament that politicians should always speak plainly or from the heart and 'tell it like it is' without the corruption of manipulative calculation or the input of professional speechwriters. This is a noble-sounding sentiment that appeals to our preference for genuineness, but where does it actually lead us?

The fight between Brutus and Antony provides the answer. While posing as 'plain blunt' speaker Antony in fact used the broader range of the orator's mesmeric skills to destroy the republic. He demonstrates the problem with what we might call 'unilateral rhetorical disarmament': in the heat of battle the enemies of democracy can't be trusted to throw away their weapons. Likewise in the duel between Barack Obama and Sarah Palin. The stakes here weren't quite as high as both, for all their differences, are believers in the democratic process and the republic (although their more extreme supporters may disagree), but Obama would have been a fool to dispense with his oratory in the face of calls from the supposedly 'plain blunt' Palin to stop orating like a celebrity. Cicero was proved correct – the good need to fight for the forum with every sword and every word. In the imaginary republic of Plato the arts of great speechmaking could be dispensed with, but in the actual republic of Cicero – and the actual world we live in today – it could not and cannot.

The ultimate illustration of this was the role played by great speeches in the defeat of Hitler himself.

We've seen in preceding chapters how after the fall of France in 1940 Churchill used stirring oratory to brace the British people for a do-or-die struggle against Nazism. It's true that, as in the case of Hitler's rise to power, Churchill's rhetoric could only tap already existing sentiment to fight on. It's also true that while Churchill used fighting words effectively to help win the Battle of Britain, they were given force by a well-organised defence. Words may be bullets, but it helped to have radar, the English Channel and Spitfires to back them up. But it was one of Churchill's least well-known speeches – to his Outer Cabinet on 28 May 1940 – that was possibly one of the turning points in the Second World War.

In the account related by historian John Lukacs, having convinced the waverers in his inner War Cabinet to his policy of fighting on alone against Hitler after the fall of France, Churchill called a meeting of all of the Ministers of Cabinet rank other than the War Cabinet members. Here's how the Labour MP Hugh Dalton recounted in his diary what his Prime Minister said:

> It was idle to think that, if we tried to make peace now, we should get better terms from Germany than if we went on and fought it out. The Germans would demand our fleet – that would be called 'disarmament' – our naval bases, and much else. We should become a slave state, though a British government which would be Hitler's puppet would be set

up – 'under Mosley or some such person.' [Oswald Mosley was the leader of the British Union of Fascists.] And where should we be at the end of all that? On the other side, we had immense reserves and advantages. Therefore he said, 'We shall go on and we shall fight it out, here or elsewhere, and if this long island story of ours is to end at last, let it end only when each of us lies choking in his own blood upon the ground.'

From Churchill's memoirs, Lukacs describes how the speech was received:

There occurred a demonstration which, considering the character of the gathering – twenty-five experienced politicians and Parliament-men, who represented all the different points of view, whether right or wrong, before the war – surprised me. Quite a number seemed to jump up from the table and came running to my chair, shouting and patting me on the back. There is no doubt that had I at this juncture faltered at all in leading this nation, I should have been hurled out of office. I was sure that every Minister was ready to be killed quite soon, and have all his family and possessions destroyed, rather than give in. In this they represented the House of Commons and almost all the people. It fell to me in these coming days and months to express their sentiments on suitable occasions. This I was able to do, because they were mine also. There was a white glow, overpowering, sublime, which ran through our island from end to end.

Lukacs concentrates on Churchill's behind-the-scenes political manoeuvring to win over the War Cabinet against the opposition of the old appeasers Neville Chamberlain and Lord Halifax. But what of the speech? Its importance was that it elicited the over-whelming support of his Outer Cabinet to prosecute the war against Hitler to the bitter end – a fact he pointedly relayed directly to his

Winston Churchill – when he spoke, people marched and fought and died.
Photo: © Popperfoto/Getty Images.

War Cabinet directly afterwards when it resumed to decide finally whether to seek negotiations with Hitler or fight on. It's probable the Outer Cabinet members were resolved to fight on anyway, but, as Churchill points out, containing as it did former appeasers and likely supporters of his Conservative Party rivals, this could not be taken for granted. In the forum that counted, Churchill's stirring oratory – with its convincing redescription of peace terms as surrender and slavery under British fascism (employing *paradiastole*), and its use of *ethos* and *pathos* to appeal to patriotism – achieved far more than the calmly logical and gentlemanly political realism of those arguing for negotiations. The substance of Churchill's Outer Cabinet speech became the theme of his subsequent addresses to the Parliament and nation for which he is most remembered.

In his collection of the great speeches in history, the former White House speechwriter William Safire recounts the saying that:

'When Pericles speaks, the people say, "How well he speaks". But when Demosthenes speaks, the people say, "Let us march!"' Churchill's oratory in 1940 was able to convince first his government and then the British people to fight on until they lay on the ground choking in their own blood – which many of them did. At perhaps the decisive moment for democracy in modern times, Winston Churchill was able to use all the weapons at the orator's disposal to inspire his audience to defend liberty from evil. There can be no greater example of the power of great oratory, and no clearer illustration of the moral necessity for democrats – whether conservative or liberal – to accept the responsibility to take the arts of speechmaking seriously.

# Chapter 9
# Gettysburg

Every speechwriter knows the feeling...

Having commissioned you with an additional, last-minute job for the next day's campaigning, the chief of staff turns to you as he's leaving your windowless, non-corner office somewhere near the photocopy room and says: 'Oh, and make it as good as the Gettysburg Address.' 'Well, when have you known me not to?'

So why is Lincoln's famous speech, delivered on 19 November 1863, regarded as the standard by which all others are judged? Most of all because of its significance in redefining what America stood for. But that's not the whole answer. Let's bring the preceding analysis together to answer the question.

*Classification*: The Gettysburg Address is a funeral oration, and a sub-genre of *epideictic* or display oratory. It follows the accepted convention set in Pericles' famous example – using the occasion of a funeral to praise the dead for their bravery and commend the way of life and the system of government for which they died.

*Forum*: The setting was a battlefield and cemetery where the decisive clash of the Civil War had occurred. The audience was not only funeral mourners but also the nation through the newspaper

Lincoln – speech etched in stone. Photo: © Kanwarjit Singh Boparai/ Shutterstock.com.

reporters present. The moment was a crucial one: a time of war-weariness when those fighting and those paying taxes needed to be reminded why. As a bloody civil war, and therefore a climactic point in the nation's history, this was the time to define the nation's essence and uniqueness.

*Ethos*: As a funeral oration, the address identified the humble, non-combatant speaker with the heroism of those who died and the values for which they died.

*Pathos*: It evokes sorrow, but in a highly restrained manner, suited to the dignity of the occasion. It is therefore not an over-whelmingly emotive speech. There is no triumphalism and no overt patriotism.

*Logos*: No facts are given about the battle; not even the numbers of the dead. As an epideictic speech, its point is not to inform or win an argument.

*Style*: It is in the *middle style* – restrained but with an obvious technical majesty. The grid below shows it to be rich in figurative speech. Although classical, it is infused with biblical rather than Greek and Roman allusion and language. The speech that preceded it on the day – by the famed orator Edward Everett – was far more self-consciously classical, but few can recall any of it (in large part because at two hours in length it was an indulgence, packed with what Cicero would have recognised as ridiculously excessive 'embroidery'). The rhetoric and wisdom were perfectly matched. It was not anachronistic but compelling, relevant and meaningful.

### Analysis of the Gettysburg Address

| Words | Style | Proof |
|---|---|---|
| Fŏur scōre \| aňd sēv \| ĕn yēars \| ăgo | *archaism; periphrasis; iambic tetrameter* | |
| our fathers brought forth on this continent a new nation, conceived in liberty, and dedicated to the proposition that all men are created equal. | *antonomasia* – allusion to the *Declaration of Independence* | *ethos* – the nation's central ideal |
| Now we are engaged in a great civil war, testing whether that nation, or any nation, so conceived and so dedicated, can long endure. | *epiphora* – repetition of 'nation' <br> *anaphora* – repetition of 'so' <br> *parallelism* – three clauses of similar construction ('so..., so..., can...') | *ethos* – this is a test of our character |
| We are met on a great battlefield of that war. | *repetition* – 'great' and 'war' from above | *forum* – the context described |
| We have come to dedicate a portion of that field, as a final resting place for those who here gave their lives that that nation might live | *repetition* – 'field' from above <br> *antanaclasis* – 'lives' changes to 'live' | *ethos* – the ideal of sacrifice for the nation |

**Analysis of the Gettysburg Address (*cont.*)**

| Words | Style | Proof |
|---|---|---|
| It is altogether fitting and proper that we should do this. | *meiosis* – understatement for dramatic effect | *ethos* – honouring the dead is a scared duty |
| But, in a larger sense, we cannot dedicate... we cannot consecrate... we cannot hallow this ground. | *anaphora* – three repetitions of 'we cannot' (also *tricolon*) *isocolon* – identical construction ('we cannot dedicate...', 'we cannot consecrate') | |
| The brave men, living and dead, who struggled here, have consecrated it, far above our poor power to add or detract. | *parallelism* – first four phrases similarly constructed *alliteration* – 'poor power' and 'add or detract' *meiosis* – 'struggled' as understatement | *ethos* – bravery, consecration and modesty *pathos* – struggled |
| The world will little note, nor long remember what we say here, but it can never forget what they did here. | *antithesis* – 'little note' versus 'long remember'; 'remember' versus 'forget'; 'we say' versus 'they did' *epiphora* – repetition of 'here' *alliteration* – 'what we' *litotes* – understatement used as a form of modesty (the world most certainly did remember what was said) | |
| It is for us the living, rather, to be dedicated here to the unfinished work which they who fought here have thus far so nobly advanced. | *epiphora* – repetition of 'here' *antithesis* – 'us' versus 'them' *antanaclasis* – 'dedicate' (from above) used in a difference sense | *ethos* – they died for freedom; the task isn't finished; their duty passes to us |

(*cont.*)

| Words | Style | Proof |
|---|---|---|
| It is rather for us to be here dedicated to the great task remaining before us – that from these honoured dead we take increased devotion to that cause for which they gave the last full measure of devotion | *anaphora* – repetition, roughly of 'rather', 'it is for us to be' <br> *repetition* – 'dedicate' again; 'devotion' <br> *parenthesis* – breaks off to describe the task | *ethos* and *pathos* – they died for us |
| – that we here highly resolve that these dead shall not have died in vain – that this nation, under God, shall have a new birth of freedom | *antanaclasis* – 'dead' changes to 'died' <br> *antithesis* – 'death' versus 'birth' | *pathos* – we mustn't let them die in vain |
| – and that government of the people, by the people, for the people, shall not perish from the earth. | *anaphora* – repetition of 'that' at beginning of four successive clauses <br> *epiphora, tricolon, isocolon, alliteration* – all in the famous last line | *ethos* – the universal human values the nation fights for |

The Gettysburg Address is unlikely to have been so well remembered if its hugely significant substance had not been matched with such sublime expression. Would we remember it if, for instance, the now universally repeatable formulation of the essence of modern democracy – 'government of the people, by the people, for the people' – had been phrased with greater exactness but less style as something like: 'our system of representative democracy, with its bicameral legislature, independent executive government and separation of powers'? The answer obviously is 'no'.

In short, the reason why the Gettysburg Address stands out is that it attains so many of Cicero's classical standards – with the right combination of character, emotion, facts and style suitable for its moment, which was one of unparalleled national significance. The *ethos* it expresses is not just American but is based on values relevant to the whole of humanity, giving it universal significance. If you want to understand great oratory, understand the Gettysburg Address.

# Chapter 10
# Speechwriter

## 1

$$\text{\reasefont{R R R}}$$

Now we examine the practical question of how a speech gets made.

As we have seen, like most things worth doing, speechwriting involves the mastery of technique. This makes it a skilled trade; but it is a special trade. Think of a carpenter: a competent one can make a chair that will remain upright when you sit on it; a great one can make a chair that will be exhibited in the Guggenheim Museum. Like a great chair a great speech will contain the essential characteristics of art: aspiration towards beauty; passion for the cause; knowledge of the subject. It requires education and belief as well as skill. It also involves a moral standpoint. It has a commercial aspect at times. Writing for diverse clients for a fee is a part of the speechwriter's life – and to the extent that commerce is inescapable and makes the world go around, perfectly justifiable. But that doesn't make speechwriting a morally neutral occupation. Words can be expressed well through the use of technique, but they can never quite be morally separated from the things they argue for. To paraphrase George Orwell, a wall that stands up is a good wall, but if it surrounds a concentration camp, it is an abomination. No speech-writer should ever use words to build such a wall. In fact, as we've seen, some of the greatest speeches are about pulling walls down. The occasional speech for a telephone company or movie studio does no harm, but for a tobacco company? For the major part of their work, speechwriters should be part of the movement they serve. A true speechwriter never writes for the political opposition. Arguing *pro* and *contra* is best left for the high school debating team. All of these characteristics – skill, artistry, knowledge, belief and moral purpose – combine to make speechwriting more than a job; they make it a vocation.

## 2

Primarily, it is a political vocation. Ever since Rob Lowe played President Bartlett's speechwriter, Sam Seaborn, on the television series *The West Wing*, students, young political advisers and others have frequently asked me how to become a speechwriter.

Rob Lowe (right) as Sam Seaborn in *The West Wing* – the speechwriter as hero. Photo: © Getty Images.

It's not an easy question to answer, partly because there is no curriculum, no course, no career path; in fact, there are few full-time jobs. The speechwriter will find him or herself writing for politicians, community leaders and company CEOs – as well as writing a lot of journalism, annual reports, policy papers and the occasional book. Few can make a living from speechwriting alone.

The best place to start is to become a candidate for office or, failing that, to join the staff of another more successful than you – the best one you can find. (The most famous speechwriters are the ones fortunate to find a great orator to employ them.) If you join a politician's staff, unless it's the office of a party leader, prime minister or president, it's unlikely you will be answering an advertisement for a speechwriter. Those jobs, as I mentioned, are rare. Once inside the office, though, if you have the inclination you will find no difficulty in gravitating towards the role. This will be for two reasons: first, because few young professionals these days know how to write; and second, because speechwriting is hard – the pure spin doctors tend to have more fun. There's also an element of what you may have seen in old Hollywood war movies: when the officers ask for a volunteer to step forward for a dangerous mission, the old hands step back, leaving you the sole applicant for the suicide squad. Should you survive, though, the rewards will be great.

# 3

Something you will notice from the back stories of the great speechwriters is their similar intellectual journey.

Whether they're from academia or journalism, they're almost certain to have history or literature majors, possess huge libraries, and be party stalwarts and true believers in their movement's cause. They also happen to be lovers of their craft. It's a case of political partisanship combined with professional pride; the two cannot be separated.

Ted Sorensen and John F. Kennedy examine a draft – it helps to write for a great politician. Photo: © Time & Life Pictures/Getty Images.

The great speechwriters need above all to have serious intellect. While they must master the ability to become instant experts on any topic – from the environment to education to the economy – good speechwriters have depth. The best are not the surface skimmers the cynics take them for. They are certainly not the mercenary hired pens of journalistic complaint. They don't just do it for the money. In this regard, they are, in their own way, a bit like Cicero himself. It's easy to imagine a Sorensen, a Noonan, a Favreau, a Freudenberg, or a Watson meeting with the Roman's ready approval.

# 4

Perhaps the greatest reward for the speechwriter is the opportunity to be at the centre of events.

I used to feel quite sorry for my old colleagues, the policy advisers, so often kept away by the senior staff from the central action, reduced to the role of battery chickens, confined to their cages, laying the policy eggs that kept the rest of us nourished. By contrast,

as the speechwriter you have to be across everything, and often get to sit in on the crucial inner meetings, watching the action unfold, and trying to get a handle on the issues, the motivations and the words being used to describe them. (That's another aspect of the speechwriting trade: few great lines are completely original; your job is to listen, absorb, re-work and repeat.)

This invitation to become an observer, though, comes with the obligation of trust. There's a time and place for the speechwriter's memoir – usually well after the major players have moved on – and speechwriters tend to write the most memorable and illuminating histories of their administrations, but there is no place for the tattle-tale, Kitty Kelly-style expose. Speechwriters are interested in the big picture.

# 5

Being an observer, though, comes with its problems, including ones Cicero can't help you with. Among them is the misapprehension that you're just there to do as you are told. Few speechwriters are able to boast as Ted Sorensen did that, 'In the Kennedy White House I *was* the senior staff member'. Often they are seen as troublemakers, gadflies, dangerous book-writing intellectuals, and bleeding hearts in a world ruled by tabloid readers and Ivy League- and Oxbridge-educated technocrats. The practical outcome is that you can be dismissed as a mere scribe. The worst leaders will treat you as a typist and will insist on writing their own speeches. This can be beneficial if they are good, but if they are not, it's the audi-ences who will suffer. These are the politicians who usually end up having nervous breakdowns – the result of spending their evenings writing speeches after spending their days running the nation.

This mistaken idea that you are just a typist manifests itself the same way in every political office: advisers will frequently expect you to use their words – even when they can't write. Stand up fights and face-to-face screaming matches that require physical separation are not unknown. And this is understandable, because the speech is the pointy end of the political office's spear; after putting so much effort into sharpening it, every member of the phalanx wants to do the stabbing.

Major speeches, for instance, follow a familiar pattern, whether you're in Downing Street, Pennsylvania Avenue or National Circuit in Canberra. After you unlock the door to your (as I've said, small and windowless) office, and circulate your initial draft, you will find you are suddenly busy and popular (this isn't always the case). Your doorway will become a favourite hangout for those wanting to exert influence. Noticing the absence of their favoured line, wonks and flacks will begin to lobby – first with charm, then with subterfuge, always with intent, always prepared to go over your head to whomever they think will help. That important paragraph on the labour law implications of the new reform – which you inexplicably left out, but which the union donors *must* hear – will cause them to declare war. If you doubt me, recall that Kennedy's foreign affairs advisers would have watered down his *Ich bin ein Berliner* speech, and that the State Department tried its best to stop Ronald Reagan telling Mr Gorbachev to tear down his wall.

Your job is clear: to listen politely and then say 'no' to anything that will undermine the success of the speech as a speech. When it comes to a speech, the role of your colleagues is to ensure that what you say is accurate and not likely to be politically counter-productive; it is not to tell you what to say, or how to say it, or to bog the delivery down in tedious and unnecessary detail. (That can be left for a press release.) The role of the speechwriter is to protect your speech as a piece of oratory – to ensure that it gets its message across, holds the audience's attention for the whole twenty minutes (seldom longer) and makes your boss look good. He or she will thank you if the speech is a success. Ride in the car on the way to the event with your speaker; don't give the speech's opponents an opening – as I did, leaving Simon Crean to the advisers on the war to the anti-war rally that helped end his career.

The preceding requires a particular attitude: you must accept that *you are the speech*. Your job isn't over when the first draft lands on the boss's desk; it's over only when the final draft appears with positive comment on the front page of the next day's newspapers.

## 6

As a speechwriter one of the first lessons you will discover is that being a speechwriter is not like being a part-time poet. It involves hard work, not just sudden inspiration. (I know one excellent speechwriter who actually is a poet, but he's the exception.) You will be bombarded regularly with requests from people to write a speech for your boss on their pet topics. These people seldom deliver; the task is harder than they think. And when there's a major speech to be written you will also be bombarded with poetic speech openings (the bit that usually gets on television). If you need such help, ask for it. If the boss wants other drafts to consider, he or she will commission them. Otherwise be wary of such 'help'. After all, you are the one who will have to stay up all night before the speech is delivered, getting it right. Have confidence in yourself. Remember, you are the speechwriter; you must take responsibility if things go wrong; *you are the speech*. And whenever you are on the outside, resist the temptation to be the guy with the great opening, because one day the job of principal speechwriter might just be yours.

## 7

Being a primarily creative endeavour, there's another very practical but essential lesson for the budding speechwriter: never compose in front of the computer screen. Doing so carries the temptation to cut and paste from policy documents and to focus too narrowly on individual sentences and lose sight of the bigger narrative. Great speeches are not based on details alone or things you can find on the internet; they are based on your beliefs, your ethics, your world view, your knowledge, your political experience and common sense, all combined with your technical rhetorical expertise.

In other words, it involves creativity and a certain moral and spiritual effort. So remove yourself from your office, go to a café, take your notebook and pen, think expansively and knock out your first draft on paper. The result will be faster, superior, more uplifting.

# 8

An important practical lesson of speechwriting is the same one Eric Liddell in *Chariots of Fire* told us about running a race: 'It's hard. It requires concentration of will, energy of soul'. You will only get a great result if you put in a supreme effort.

You have to invest the necessary time and sweat into the crucial parts of the speech. In this book I have set out ten important elements common to great speeches. Few great speeches include all ten, but none omit them all. The speechwriter must ask him or herself the following questions as they write their speech – and then expend blood, toil, tears and sweat before answering 'yes' to each one:

1   *Forum*: Who is the audience and do I understand their likely reactions to what I am going to write?
2   *Handshake*: Have I really grabbed them and connected with them? Will they have a good reason to keep listening after the opening sentence?
3   *Purpose*: What is the purpose of the speech? Have I stated it directly, without equivocation? Have I explained why it is important?
4   *Message and sound bite*: What's the message I want them to take home? What's the standout line I want them to repeat to others? Does it have a technical quality that makes it shine?
5   *Facts*: What's the killer fact I want them to repeat to others? Have I focused the spotlight on its importance?
6   *Refutation*: Have I demolished the other side's arguments and credibility?

7 *Emotion*: Have I explored the obvious emotional potentialities of the speech and succeeded in tapping the audience's
emotions? Have I included stories, metaphors and other
devices?

8 *Character*: Have I reflected and projected the winning features of the speaker's character? Will they believe he or she
is telling the truth if it comes down to 'he said, she said'?

9 *Structure*: Does the speech have a logical coherence? More
importantly, have I kept the audience's attention?

10 *Conclusion*: Have I maintained the quality to the end? Does
it end on a high by tapping the emotions once more or by
re-stating the case with overwhelming force?

# 9

Now that you've done these ten things, the success of your speech
is dependent upon one thing the speechwriter can't fully control –
or as Demosthenes put it *three* things: delivery, delivery and again
delivery (which by now you will recognise as a *tricolon*, with *repetition*, etc.). Cicero agreed, and his own delivery was, by all accounts,
magnificent. He called it 'a sort of language of the body, since it
consists of movement or gesture as well as of voice or speech'.
In other words, he regarded oratory as a political variation on
acting.

This is something about which the speechwriter can do little,
except choose clients well, or have the good fortune to be there
when a new star emerges. The Sorensens, the Noonans, the Favreaus
and the Freudenbergs have all the luck! Not for them the urge to
climb the stage, fight the speaker for the microphone and deliver
the speech themselves.

But it is something about which candidates for office can do a
great deal, especially if they begin young.

The speech coach can help the poor orator improve, but having
worked with a few, I'm convinced that by the time they are in a

position to employ a speechwriter, politicians have either 'got it' or they haven't. A pessimist would suggest that speaking well is a skill you are born with, and there's little we can do about it. Certainly, the right sort of voice helps; and in this regard Obama and John F. Kennedy were blessed. But many great speakers, like Demosthenes, Churchill and the great Welsh Labour Party orator Aneurin Bevan, were stutterers. This tells us that great orators aren't born; they're made.

Like most difficult skills, eloquence involves initial training, followed by practice, especially if you want to hold an audience of 80 000 in a packed stadium or a million in front of the Lincoln Memorial. Demosthenes, for instance, trained to make his voice stronger by talking with pebbles in his mouth. Cicero overcame a weak voice through a training regime so thorough and impressive that even the fathers of his fellow students would come to school to hear him declaim. As we have seen in this book, the techniques of successful oratory have been well understood since classical times. We know they work. What the orator needs is experience in using them, and the confidence to recognise what's likely to work in particular situations. It's this lack of confidence to deliver lines well that usually causes a speaker to put the red pencil through what are potentially the best lines of a script.

Modest speakers can have success by staying within their limitations to deliver speeches with brevity, sincerity and dignity. Grand orators have to take calculated risks, and it's best to gain a feel for the odds of success *before* you reach the nominating convention – a mistake Bill Clinton made in 1988, when he bored the audience so badly while nominating Michael Dukakis that they cheered when he said, 'In conclusion'. A good speaker therefore needs to know how to:

- adopt the tone of voice appropriate for each a particular subject and each particular audience
- send response cues to the audience to laugh at jokes, applaud sound bites and reply to rhetorical questions

- avoid speaking in a monotone and modulate the voice appropriately throughout a speech to evoke humour, emotion and intimacy
- control his or her movement and get hand gestures and facial expressions right
- do all the above and more without seeming as if you are acting.

The last point is crucial. Audiences can see through a faker.

Good delivery shouldn't be used to make demagoguery easier; it should help speakers to project the full force of what their speech contains. And in the same way that an architect designs better buildings by understanding what engineers do, a speechwriter writes better speeches by understanding what actors and their speakers have to do.

## 10

Ultimately, the tasks you set for your speech and the techniques you employ to fulfil them must answer this question: does the effect add up to more than the sum of the techniques employed? Does it have a vital ingredient? One which an adviser to Tony Blair once pithily expressed to me as 'edge, crunch, lift' (yes, employing a *tricolon* and *isocolon*!). Is it sharp? Is it strong? Can it raise the audience and our democracy to a higher level? Does it, like a speech from John F. Kennedy, try to inspire 'energy, faith, devotion' to solving the problems of the world? Do you, the speechwriter, believe in it? Is it really, truly worthwhile, not a smartly presented set of debating tactics? Have you put your speech into the hands of an orator who is morally worthy of it and able to make it sing? If you can answer 'yes' to those questions, you've fulfilled your debt to Cicero and made his sacrifice to save the Republic worthwhile.

# Conclusion: The ideal orator

In this book we've seen many great orators at work, some engaged in notable rhetorical duels: between Brutus and Antony for the future of the Roman Republic; between Churchill and Hitler for the future of the world; and between Obama and Palin for the future of the modern United States. We've looked at the elements of the DNA of speech and the way that the belief and passion of speakers and speechwriters bring that DNA to life. And we've looked at Cicero's conception of the ideal orator. Let's conclude by answering the question: Who among the orators we have looked at represents the ideal? Who is the best?

We know who Cicero would have chosen – Cicero. He may have been right. But for the sake of argument, let's exclude him and look at the competition. And for the sake of brevity, let's break down our analysis into three categories representing in broad terms the qualities Cicero himself would have looked for:

- **technique** – employment of figures, rhythm and logic
- **substance** – knowledge and moral purpose
- **passion** – projection of emotion, character and sheer fighting spirit.

**Comparison of qualities in orators' speeches**

|  | Technique | Substance | Passion |
|---|---|---|---|
| Mark Antony | • |  | • |
| Marcus Brutus | • | • |  |
| Winston Churchill | • | • | • |
| Adolf Hitler | • |  | • |
| John F. Kennedy | • | • | • |

(cont.)

|                      | Technique | Substance | Passion |
|----------------------|:---------:|:---------:|:-------:|
| Bobby Kennedy        |           | •         | •       |
| Martin Luther King   | •         | •         | •       |
| Sarah Palin          | •         |           | •       |
| Barack Obama         | •         | •         | •       |

What can we conclude?

**Marcus Brutus** demonstrates that you can have a polished style and a laudable purpose but still fail in your essential task of victory by being unprepared to fight with every available weapon for control of the forum. He should have listened to Cicero.

**Mark Anthony** proves that sometimes ruthlessness, energy and passion can outpoint technical perfection, character and logic, but his moral failings – exposed so witheringly by Cicero – exclude him from the final list.

**Adolf Hitler** was able to work an audience like no other. In rousing the negative emotions he is unsurpassed on our list. But his intellectual shallowness and the evilness of his demagoguery would have appalled Cicero as much as it appalls us. A great orator cannot be evil.

**Sarah Palin** wins on folksiness and charm and has a fighting spirit perhaps superior to any contemporary rival, but she lacks – yet – the necessary knowledge of the world and political judgement to be regarded as a stateswoman and ideal orator.

**Bobby Kennedy** wins the category of substance, thanks to the thoughtful and provoking speeches made during his doomed presidential campaign. His willingness to speak, despite the dangers it entailed, makes him in some ways the equal of the mature Cicero, author of the Philippics. Technically, though, he is perhaps the least impressive of our great orators.

This leaves us with four contenders who achieve a perfect score.

Winston Churchill was a master of the English language, whose sound bites remain some of the most memorable sentences of any age. His speeches are rich in historical and literary understanding – qualities which enabled them to identify and exploit the urgency of the moment in 1940. While his delivery was flat by comparison with others on our list, his *middle style* was perfectly suited to the forum of the House of Commons. The passion is demonstrated in his evocation of patriotism and the fact that, had he failed, death likely awaited.

Martin Luther King combined technical excellence, richness of content, passion and moral force in a southern preaching style that exploited the potentialities of biblical metaphor better than any other. His courage was beyond question: more exposed than Churchill, death awaited and caught up with him. And his achievements as the most important leader of the modern civil rights movement, which inspired similar freedom movements around the world, prove what great oratory can achieve.

Barack Obama has almost single-handedly created a resurgence of interest in oratory. His addresses are textbook examples of figurative speech. His ability to hold an audience is matched only by Martin Luther King and Jesse Jackson. By overcoming the fact of his race and the past failings of his party, and by using speech to take on the most vexed issues of the times – and win the argument! – Obama had demonstrated that words cannot only make a statesman, they can potentially remake a country, as Lincoln did in the nineteenth century.

John F. Kennedy *is* speech. Helped by the master speechwriter Ted Sorensen, Kennedy's speeches provide the ultimate examples of the use of classical figurative technique. They are steeped in patriotic *ethos* – the rich legacy of Lincoln and of Kennedy's own life as a war hero – and contained the perfect level of passion apt for the circumstances he faced and the office he held. Few could project purpose as clearly and in doing so instill confidence and resolve in his audiences. He could construct and hold a forum with ease. But while his language was poetic, it was eloquence matched by wisdom – demonstrated by the fact that in its hour of need he and his generation had the intellectual capacities and judgement needed to save the world from potential nuclear annihilation.

So what is our verdict? Any one of the last four could be hailed as an ideal orator in the absence of others. All used oratory bravely to seize a moment to achieve great things – defeat tyranny, promote freedom, make the impossible dream of an African-American presidency come true, and put wisdom into the White House in a time of nuclear standoff. Each had or still has their own technical strengths; not just mastery of figurative language and prose rhythm but also the proofs of rhetoric: Churchill *ethos* through historical allusion; King *pathos* through metaphor; and Obama *pathos* through parable, and *logos* through historical exposition. This perhaps is what separates them, because for mastery across so many areas of technique – holding a forum, using language, projecting character, appealing to positive human emotions and arguing a logical case – Kennedy was supreme. John F. Kennedy is my choice for Cicero's mantle of ideal orator of the world. Who is yours?

# Appendix

# Common figures and terms

## Figurative speech

There are thousands of techniques for speaking figuratively, and many have multiple names and many subtle variations. The following is a brief but I hope useful list of some of the most commonly observed figurative devices.

**Schemes**: calculated differences in the way words are arranged to make them more attractive or give them greater force

- *accumulation*: a vigorous summation of previous points
- *alliteration*: beginning a series of words with the same letter or a similar sound
- *anadiplosis*: beginning a clause or sentence with the last or most prominent word of the preceding sentence
- *anaphora*: beginning successive clauses, sentences or paragraphs with the same word or words
- *antimetabole* (also 'chiasmus'): repetition of words in successive clauses but in (rough) reverse order

- *antithesis*: the employment of opposite or contrasting ideas
- *aposiopesis*: breaking off from a speech suddenly for dramatic effect
- *apostrophe*: sudden redirection of the speech to another person or object
- *assonance*: the use of two or more words that sound similar
- *asyndeton*: the exclusion of conjunctions between words or clauses (usually the omission of 'and' in lists)
- *climax*: words or ideas arranged in escalating importance
- *epanalepsis*: beginning or ending a clause or sentence with the same word or words
- *epiphora*: repetition of the same word or words at the end of a clause or sentence
- *isocolon*: a succession of phrases containing an equal number of syllables
- *parallelism*: the use of two or more similarly constructed clauses
- *parenthesis*: interrupting a sentence to introduce additional descriptive information
- *periphrasis*: using multiple words when one or two will do
- *polysyndeton*: the multiple use of conjunctions in rapid succession
- *repetition*: repeating words or clauses for forceful effect
- *symploce*: the combination of *anaphora* and *epiphora* in the same line.
- *tricolon*: speaking in threes to emphasise points.

**Tropes**: changes in the normally accepted meaning of words

- *allegory*: storytelling employed as a metaphor
- *allusion*: indirect reference to a person, thing or event
- *antanaclasis*: repetition of a word whose meaning changes
- *anthimeria*: the substitution of one part of speech for another (e.g. nouns as verbs, nouns as adjectives, etc.)

- *anthypophora*: asking and then immediately answering rhetorical questions
- *antiphrasis*: using words opposite to their usual meaning
- *antonomasia*: the substitution of a descriptive phrase for a name and vice versa
- *archaism*: the use of outdated words
- *commiseration*: invoking pity
- *ellipsis*: intentional omission of details
- *erotema*: asking a rhetorical question
- *hyperbole:* intentional exaggeration, not meant to be taken literally
- *innuendo*: using words to convey an indirect, usually disparaging, meaning
- *irony*: using words to express the opposite of their usual meaning
- *litotes*: a form of irony that employs understatement, usually by stating the negative of the contrary (e.g. 'it was no small accomplishment')
- *maxim*: a pithily expressed precept relating or moral or political behaviour
- *meiosis*: deliberate understatement to reduce importance
- *metaphor*: substituting one thing for another to describe an object, happening or action more vividly
- *oxymoron*: using two words with opposite meanings to make a contradictory statement
- *parable*: an extended metaphor, usually in the form of a story, to make a moral point
- *paradiastole*: the rhetorical re-description of something to give it lesser or greater significance, or more positive or negative qualities than your opponent has claimed
- *paradox*: posing a contradiction to evoke a truth
- *paronomasia*: a pun using similar sounding words with differing meanings
- *personification*: attributing human agency to non-human objects or events

- *praeteritio*: alluding to something while pretending to pass over it
- *pysma*: asking multiple rhetorical questions
- *satire*: using sarcasm, irony or ridicule to highlight vice or folly or to send up opponents
- *simile*: comparing two or more things
- *syncatabasis*: the art of speaking at the level of your audience
- *topos (pl. topoi)*: common forms of argumentation.

## Aristotle's proofs

*Character (ethos)*: the creation of trust in what the speaker says by identifying with the values and beliefs of the audience or the characteristic spirit of the age or community

*Emotion (pathos)*: the successful appeal to the audience's emotions

*Logic (logos)*: the logical coherency of the speaker's case, backed by the right facts.

## Classifications

*Forensic*: a legal speech in a law court

*Deliberative*: a political speech in an executive council, legislature or public assembly

*Display*: a speech in praise of others, such as a eulogy, or a formal occasion for 'showing off' the speaker's eloquence.

## Divisions

*Prologue (exordium)*: the opening remarks that grab the audience's attention and sympathies

*Narrative*: the speaker's major contention or case

*Proofs*: the arguments used to support the speaker's contention or case

*Refutation*: refuting the arguments of the opposing case

*Conclusion (peroration)*: summing up or ending by cinching the case or ramming the major points home.

# Canons

*Invention*: the discovery of useful arguments (what to say)

*Disposition*: the arrangement of the arguments for maximum effect (how to set it out)

*Elocution*: employing the right rhetorical style to give the delivery extra force (how to say it)

*Memory*: recall – crucial in the age before the word processor and the autocue (how to remember it without reading)

*Pronunciation*: delivery ('how to deliver it on the night').

# Styles

*Plain style*: a direct and concise way of speaking, stripped of all obvious rhythm, ornament and emotion; designed to be clear rather than impressive; sometimes intentionally delivered to sound untrained

*Middle style*: emphasises argument and content; can contain *tropes* and schemes, and can contain emotion, but in a restrained way; charming rather than vigorous

*Grand style*: the most forceful style of speaking in which the power of the argument is matched by the majesty of the diction; employs every relevant oratorical device to arouse the audience and sway its emotions; can be rough and severe, smooth and charming, or high toned and principled, depending on the needs of the speaker

*Stentorian*: loudly sounding a call to duty or sacrifice

*Extempore*: speaking impromptu, without preparation, off the cuff

*Invective*: violent verbal attack

*Pastoral*: idealising simple, rural life.

# Notes

## Introduction

p. 1 '10 out of 10... delivery' *Australian*, 30 August 2008.

p. 3 'In 161 BC... city', *Oxford Classical Dictionary*, 3rd edn, ed. Simon Hornblower and Anthony Spawforth, Oxford.

p. 4 'How can intelligent... media', Geoffrey Barker, *Australian Financial Review*, 3 May 2010.

## Chapter 1 – To save a republic

p. 10 'falling, according to... statue', Appian, *The Civil Wars*, trans. John Carter, Penguin, Harmondsworth, 1996, p. 132.

pp. 10–11 'But on the 17th... players', Plutarch, *Makers of Rome*, trans. Ian Scott-Kilvert, Harmondsworth, London, 1975, pp. 238–9.

p. 11 'Romans,' he said,... slaves', Appian, *The Civil Wars*, pp. 143–6.

pp. 11–12 'In this inspired... anger', Appian, *The Civil Wars*, pp. 148–9.

p. 12 'As soon as he saw ... alight', Plutarch, *Makers of Rome*, p. 240.

p. 14 'By the middle... philosophy', Quentin Skinner, *Reason and Rhetoric in the Philosophy of Hobbes*, Cambridge University Press, Cambridge, 1996, p. 23; Brian Vickers, *In Defence of Rhetoric*, Oxford University Press, Oxford, 1989, p. 256.

p. 14 'Ovid, Virgil... others', Skinner, *Reason and Rhetoric*, pp. 21 and 27; Park Honan, *Shakespeare: A Life*, Oxford University Press, Oxford, 1998, pp. 53–4.

pp. 14–15 'In the summer... violence', Stephen Greenblatt, *Will in the World: How Shakespeare became Shakespeare*, Jonathan Cape, London, 2004, p. 26.

p. 15 'first form... Greek', Skinner, *Reason and Rhetoric*, p. 27.

p. 21 'The *New York Times*... better', *New York Times*, 29 August 2009.

pp. 25–6 'he was regarded as... stabbing', Antony Everitt, *Cicero: The life and times of Rome's greatest politician*, Random House, New York, 2001, p. 269, pp. 274–5.

p. 27 'Thanks to a combination... made', *Oxford English dictionary*, p. 1560.

p. 27 'The voice of Hortensius... Republic', Cicero, *Brutus*, ed. and trans. G.L. Henderson, Loeb, London, 2001, pp. 287.

pp. 28–9 'we demand the acuteness... profession', Cicero, 'On the orator', in *On the good life*, ed. and trans. Michael Grant, Penguin, London, 1971, p. 280.

p. 29 'A *vir bonus*... office', Skinner, *Reason and Rhetoric*, p. 74.

p. 29 'His eloquence... demand', Cicero, 'On the orator', p. 307.

p. 30 'the best speakers... ruin', Cicero, 'On the orator', p. 249.

p. 31 'you are bereft... you', Cicero, *Brutus* (Loeb edition), p. 289.

pp. 32–3 'Would you like us... country!', Cicero, 'The second philippic against Antony', in *Selected Works*, ed. and trans. Michael Grant, Penguin, Harmondsworth, 1960, pp. 122, 126, 150, 152–3.

### Chapter 2 – Speech – the essence of democracy

p. 37 'When the drums beat . . . vindicated', Graham Freudenberg, *A figure of speech*, Wiley, 2005, p. 66.

p. 37 'one of the formative . . . education', *Oxford Classical Dictionary*, p. 1561.

p. 39 'A quick survey . . . important', *Oxford Classical Dictionary*, various entries.

p. 42 'betrayal of his friends . . . gods', Josiah Ober, *Mass and Elite in Democratic Athens*, Princeton University Press, Princeton N.J., 1989, p. 138; Charles Freeman, *The Greek Achievement: The foundation of the Western world*, Penguin, London, 1999, p. 227.

pp. 44–5 '[Y]ou shall hear . . . sort', Plato, the excerpts from Plato's Apology are adapted from *The Loeb Classical Library, Plato, Volume 1, Euthyphro; Apology; Crito; Phaedo; Phaedrus*; trans. Harold North Fowler, Harvard University Press, Cambridge, MA, 1914.

p. 46 'Certainly the failure . . . idealist', Mary Beard, 'Lucky city', *London Review of Books*, vol. 23, no. 16.

pp. 47–9 'Cicero was fiddling . . . moment', Robert Harris, *Lustrum*, Hutchinson, London, 2009, pp. 183–4.

p. 52 '100 minae . . . or $290 000', *The Greek Sophists*, trans. and ed. John Dillon and Tania Gergel, Penguin, London, 2003, Introduction, p. xii.

p. 53 '[6] For either it was . . . free' *The Greek Sophists*, 'The encomium of Helen', trans. and ed. John Dillon and Tania Gergel, Penguin, London, 2003, pp. 78–9.

p. 53 'Protagoras from Abdera . . . Elis', *The Greek sophists*, pp. 11, 43–4; *Greek Political Oratory*, trans. and ed. A.N.W. Saunders, Harmondsworth, London, 1987, p. 10; Freeman, *The Greek Achievement*, pp. 228–9.

p. 54 'Lysias, forced to sell . . . BC', Aristotle, *The Art of Rhetoric*, p. 5.

p. 57 'can discuss commonplace . . . style', Cicero, 'On the Orator', pp. 357, 379.

p. 58 'a man of the highest . . . discernment', *Oxford Classical Dictionary*, p. 1290.

p. 58 'it became a guiding . . . society', Quentin Skinner, *The Foundations of Modern Political Thought, Vol. 1, The Renaissance*, Cambridge University Press, Cambridge, 1978, pp. 84–5, 88.

### Chapter 3 – Forum

p. 62 'An expert who . . . court' Cicero, 'The Brutus', in Cicero, *On Government*, trans. Michael Grant, Penguin, Harmondsworth, 1993, pp. 283–4.

p. 66 'To be ignorant . . . child' Cicero, *Orator*, p. 395.

p. 67 'by a clear head . . . part', Roy Jenkins, *Churchill*, Pan, London, 2001, pp. 576–8.

p. 67 'by playing on . . . today', Jenkins, *Churchill*, p. 578.

p. 68 'I had rather . . . nothing else.', Christopher Hill, *God's Englishman*, Penguin, Harmondsworth, 1979, p. 64.

pp. 68–9 'I looked up . . . the Government', Jenkins, *Churchill*, p. 579.

p. 69 'Somehow or other . . . *name of God, go.*', *House of Commons Debates*, 7 May 1940, vol. 360, pp. 1150–1.

p. 70 'Lloyd George told Amery . . . day', Jenkins, *Churchill*, p. 581.

p. 72 'As I flew over . . . continent', Terry Coleman, *Olivier*, Bloomsbury, London, 2005, pp. 155–71.

p. 78 'On a visit to Berlin . . . Berlin Wall', Robert Dallek, *John F. Kennedy: An unfinished life 1917–1963*, Penguin, London, 2004, pp. 624–6; Robert Schlesinger, *White House Ghosts: Presidents and their speechwriters from F.D.R. to George W. Bush*, Simon & Schuster, New York, 2008, pp.138–41; Ted Sorensen, *Counselor: A life at the edge of history*, HarperCollins, New York, 2009, pp. 322–5.

p. 81 'Peggy Noonan frequently...knows it', Schlesinger, *White House ghosts*, p. 345.

p. 82 'Amid the recounting...wall', Schlesinger, *White House ghosts*, pp. 354–58.

p. 83 Reagan's own handwritten...transcript, James Mann, *The Rebellion of Ronald Reagan: A history of the end of the Cold War*, Viking, New York, 2009, pp. 198, 206.


## Chapter 4 – Style

p. 90 '*Propeterea quot prudential*...suspect', Cicero, *Orator*, pp. 418–19.

p. 95 'the decision as to...it', Cicero', *Orator*, p. 441.

p. 96 'The significance...convincing', Cicero, 'The Brutus', Penguin edition, p. 265.

p. 96 'the sound bite...most', Peggy Noonan, *What I Saw at the Revolution: A political life in the Reagan era*, Random House, New York, 1990, pp. 70–1.

p. 97 'It was pretty emotional...mood', Alastair Campbell, *The Blair Years: Extracts from the Alastair Campbell diaries*, Hutchinson, London, 2007, pp. 231–3.

p. 99 'the reversible raincoat' Sorensen, *Counselor*, p. 139.

p. 100 'Your lines are garbage...good', Bill Nicholson, Speech at the launch of the International Screenwriters' Festival, 30 January 2006, www.screenwritersfestival.com/news.php?id=3, retrieved 20 May 2010.

p. 108 'If they have...intended', Cicero, *Orator*, p. 443.

p. 111 'Cicero was adamant...thought', Cicero, *Orator*, p. 445.

p. 113 'If you use...sincerity', Cicero, *Orator*, p. 481.

p. 113 'embroidery' Cicero, *Orator*, p. 455.

p. 113 'can possess...vigour', Cicero, *Orator*, p. 501.

p. 114 'In Flanders fields...fields', Schlesinger, *White House Ghosts*, p. 340.

p. 122 'a bunny-hugging vegan...words', Sarah Palin, *Going Rogue*, HarperCollins, New York, 2009, pp. 239–40.


## Chapter 5 – Emotion

pp. 125–6 'At this point...audience', John Heilemann and Mark Halperin, *Race of a Lifetime: How Obama won the White House*, Viking, New York, 2010, p. 350.

pp. 126–7 'do not seem...opposite', Aristotle, *The Art of Rhetoric*, p. 141.

pp. 127–8 'there is one way...duty' Harper Lee, *To Kill a Mockingbird*, Arrow Books, London, 2006, pp. 226–7.

p. 128 'the real quality...obtains', Cicero, 'The Brutus', Penguin, p. 278.

p. 128 'When someone is...orator', Cicero, 'The Brutus' Penguin, pp. 278, 279.

p. 129 'Aristotle lists ten...more', Aristotle, *The Art of Rhetoric*, pp. 142–71

p. 134 'It's little wonder...crying', Stewart Burns, *To the Mountaintop: Martin Luther King and his sacred mission to save America 1955–1968*, Harper Collins, New York, 2004, pp. 212, 442–4.

p. 140 'to just pinch...part', Palin, *Going Rogue*, p. 240.

p. 152 'The crowd broke up...assassination', Thurston Clarke, *The Last Campaign: Robert F. Kennedy and 82 days that inspired America*, Henry Holt and Co., New York, 2008. On the Indianapolis speech, see pp. 91–9.

### Chapter 6 – Character

p. 155 'we more readily...maintained', Aristotle, *The Art of Rhetoric*, pp. 74–5.

p. 157 'As Klein adds...campaigning', Joe Klein, *Politics Lost*, Doubleday, New York, 2006, pp.145–6.

p. 165 'As Klein says...name', Klein, *Politics Lost*, pp. 218–19.

p. 166 'Again, as Klein...being', Klein, *Politics Lost*, p. 158.

p. 172 'I felt it was...issue', Interview with Davis Guggenheim, www.aintitcool.com/node/23547, retrieved 26/01/2010.

p. 174 'Kennedy had told...inspiration', Schlesinger, *White House Ghosts*, pp.104–11; William Safire, *Lend Me Your Ears: Great speeches in history*, revised and expanded edition, W.W. Norton, New York, 1997, pp. 891–2.

### Chapter 7 – Evidence

pp. 194–5 'Now you all know...Crassus', Harris, *Lustrum*, Hutchinson, London, 2009, pp. 49–50.

p. 196 'Comparisons with...attempted', Don Watson, *Recollections of a Bleeding Heart: A portrait of Paul Keating PM*, Knopf, Sydney, 2002, pp. 288–91.

p. 200 'This is why...president', Heilemann and Halperin, *Race of a Lifetime, How Obama won the White House*, Viking, New York, 2010, p. 237.

### Chapter 8 – Morality

p. 210 'Look over this way...ever', Aristophanes, 'The clouds', in *Lysistrata and Other Plays*, translated with an introduction and notes by Alan H. Somerstein, revised edition, Penguin, London, 2002, pp. 78–9.

pp. 211–12 'While conventional right-wing ...psyche', Richard J. Evans, *The Coming of the Third Reich*, Penguin, London, 2003, pp. 171–2.

p. 212 'there was only...him', Richard J. Evans, *The Coming of the Third Reich*, Penguin, London, 2003, pp. 171–2, 224.

pp. 212–13 'Without an audience...nothing', Laurence Rees, *The Nazis: A warning from history*, BBC Books, London, 1997, pp. 35–6.

pp. 215–16 'On a scarlet-draped...syntax', George Orwell, *1984*, Penguin, London, 1981, pp. 148–9.

p. 219 'There occurred...end', John Lukacs, *Five days in London: May 1940*, Yale University Press, New Haven, 1999, pp. 3, 5.

p. 221 'When Pericles speaks...march!', William Safire, *Lend Me Your Ears*, p. 25.

### Chapter 10 – Speechwriter

p. 232 'in the Kennedy...member', Sorensen, *Counselor*, ch. 12.

p. 250 'a sort of...speech', Cicero, *Orator*, p. 347.

# Index

radio, 30, 96
referencing, 77
styles to suit, 30, 50, 51
television, 21, 23, 60, 96, 131, 156,
    178
understanding, 23, 37, 49, 56, 60,
    64, 65, 82, 135, 211, 222, 235
voters, 23, 41, 128, 149, 157–8, 173,
    187
winning their trust, 189
authenticity, 62, 112, 129, 148, 193,
    214, 217
Axelrod, David, 125

back stories, 22, 170
balance, 36, 78
Beatitudes, 98
Beatles, the, 52, 116
Beckham, David, 1
belief, 84, 136, 168, 181, 193, 212,
    228–9, 234, 239
Benn, Tony, 16
Berlin, 78–88
Bevan, Aneurin, 237
Biden, Joe, 101
Blair, Tony, 52, 96–7, 106, 107
Boston Consulting, 54
Brando, Marlon, 17
Brown, Gordon, 1, 106
Brutus, Marcus Junius, 6, 9, 10–12,
    16–17, 22, 26, 28, 30–1, 34, 91–5,
    116, 121, 123, 143, 144, 148, 152,
    217, 239, 240
Bundy, McGeorge, 78
Bush, George W., 65, 111–12, 122, 157
Bush, presidents, 159

Caesar, Julius, 6, 8–12, 15–18, 25, 26,
    28, 32, 36
calculation, 10, 20, 23
    *See also* spontaneity
Calwell, Arthur, 37, 63
Cameron, David, 107–8
Capitol, the, 9, 10, 11, 21
Catilina, Lucius Sergius, 27, 46–9
Cato, Marcus Porcius, 47
character, 6, 25, 29, 37, 56, 58, 64,
    140, 154–87, 189, 192, 203, 208,
    227, 236, 239, 242
  components of, 159
  definition, 56
  destroying opponent's, 42, 163, 165
  establishing and defending, 157, 159,
    165
  exploiting, 156
  failing to project, 166
  projecting, 6, 156, 172
  reputation, 156
  *See also* ethos

character test, failing, 162
*Chariots of Fire*, 130, 235
Charleson, Ian, 130–1
charm, 18, 30, 56, 155, 216, 240
Cheney, Dick, 163
Chifley, Ben, 135
Churchill, Winston, 6, 32, 46, 72,
    74–7, 105, 115, 191, 193–4, 215,
    218–21, 237, 239, 241, 242
Cicero, Marcus Tullius, 4, 5, 6, 7, 15,
    16, 25–34, 35–8, 39, 42, 46–9, 53,
    56, 57, 58, 60, 62, 66, 90, 91, 93,
    95, 96, 108, 111, 113, 116, 123,
    126, 128–30, 131, 137, 139, 152,
    153, 158, 159, 167, 173, 177, 187,
    194, 208, 218, 224, 226, 231,
    236–8, 239–40, 242
Cinna, Lucius Cornelius, 10
circumstances, 62
Cleon, 42
climax, 68, 91, 212
  definition, 93
  examples, 70, 87, 93, 119
Clinton, Hillary, *see* Rodham Clinton
Clinton, William Jefferson, 46, 237
Coalition Government, Australian, 158
Coleridge, Samuel Taylor, 36
Comitium, 9, 41
commiseration, 94
concern, 158
conclusions
  of speeches, 51, 130, 139, 189, 236,
    237
  *See also* peroration
Conservative Party, British, 105, 106,
    107, 188
conservatives, 5, 221
  Australian, 82
  US, 19, 149, 176, 180
content, 1, 241
contrast, 25
conviction, 5, 23
Corax, 52
courage, 32, 37, 45, 64, 74, 82, 104,
    153, 159, 189, 190, 192, 195,
    197–8, 240, 241
court of public opinion, 56, 172
Crassus, Lucius Licinius, 30
Crean, Simon, 63–5, 233
crediblity, 166
Cromwell, Oliver, 67–9
Crowe, Russell, 100
cynicism, 5, 55

dactylic, 109
Dean, Howard, 102–3
decorum
  definition, 62
  example, 69